THERAPY DOGS
AND THE
STORIES THEY
TELL

Black and White Edition

Diana F. Lee, M.Ed., M.P.A., PMCTS

Edited by
Stanley D. Wilson, Ph.D.

ISBN: 1523901659
ISBN 13: 9781523901654

Diana F. Lee, M.Ed., M.P.A., PMC Transforming Spirituality
Author of:

Rustproof Relationships: A Guide to Healthy Relationships
and Effective Communication Skills

Touching the Soul: A Therapeutic Guide to Spiritual and Personal Growth

No matter how close we are to another person, few human relationships are as free from strife, disagreement, and frustration as is the relationship you have with a good dog. Few human beings give of themselves to another as a dog gives of itself. I also suspect that we cherish dogs because their unblemished souls make us wish—consciously, or unconsciously—that we were as innocent as they are and make us yearn for a place where innocence is universal and where the meanness, the betrayals, and the cruelties of this world are unknown.

—Dean Koontz

ACKNOWLEDGMENTS

❋ ❋ ❋

There are a number of people I would like to thank for assisting in the delivery of this book. Much appreciation to my wonderful editor, Stanley D. Wilson, Ph.D., a friend who has spent much creative time and effort with me in discussing and honing the ideas I have passed along to my readers. I'd also like to mention Sue Keacher, M.Ed., Kathryn Anderson, Andrea Adams, D.N., Steve Olsen, N.D., Jennifer White (trainer), the support of my co-workers in our office building, especially Judith Milner, M.D., M.Ed., SpecEd, Pam Roberson, Dale Sobotka, M.D., Melissa Haufman, LICSW, William Taylor (supportive husband), all of whom have provided invaluable feedback about my raw manuscript. Many of my clients have made positive suggestions about the information that now appears in this book and have thus contributed to its development. A special acknowledgment is reserved for Angela Chase, who has dedicated herself to the project and made a number of creative contributions.

DEDICATION

To Jenny Lee Taylor for her loving, dedicated service as a therapy dog. She passed away at the age of fourteen after steadfastly giving her love, support, and attention to clients who suffered abuse or trauma.

ABOUT THE EXAMPLES IN THIS BOOK

None of the examples presented in this book reflect the life experiences of any one individual. Rather, each is a composite formed from the lives of numerous people I have known and treated. By using composites, changing names, and altering the stories I have heard and experienced, I protect the confidentiality of others. Any resemblance between persons I have known and real people is coincidental.

A note about pronouns: throughout the book I use "he" and "she" interchangeably to refer to the typical child or adult. Any gender reference in the text is equally applicable to either gender. Using the more modern and generic "he/she" feels unnatural to the flow of thought. Hence the reader may assume that, unless otherwise stated, any reference to one gender also holds true for the other.

TARGET POPULATION

This book is written for anyone using or considering using therapy dogs in a counseling or psychotherapy practice. It will also appeal to dog lovers in general. While geared primarily to situations involving the counseling office, it is also appropriate for application in other settings—namely, courtrooms, hospitals, nursing homes, school counseling departments, veteran centers, places of business, home visitations, hotels, libraries, church offices, etc. This book contains mature subject matter and could activate strong feelings. It uses examples of clients' issues in counseling and may not be appropriate for young children or adults who might find themselves triggered by references to abuse or trauma.

TABLE OF CONTENTS

❄ ❄ ❄

Man himself cannot express love and humility by external signs so plainly as does a dog, when with dropping ears, hanging lips, flexuous body, and wagging tail, he meets his beloved master.

—Charles Darwin

Diana Lee and Dr. Jerry

I

THE EXPERIENCE OF WORKING WITH THERAPY DOGS

The experience of working with therapy dogs delights me. I am honored to share my office and time with my canine companions, a trio of Brussels Griffons who serve as my assistants. Their personalities, sensitivities, and playfulness brighten my workdays and lighten the emotional loads of my clients. They help to keep me emotionally balanced and happy, no matter how stressful the issues my clients present.

Other professionals in my building look forward to seeing my therapy dogs, as do the clients of other therapists who share office space. Coworkers smile predictably when I enter a room with one or two of the dogs leading the way. When I choose to leave them at home—such as on a day that is too hot, or when I have too many errands to run before or after work, or if one of the dogs is not feeling well—I expect to be asked about their whereabouts and their well-being. When I show up alone, I expect to hear my clients express disappointment, as they depend on having them in the room. More than once a client's disappointment was so heavy that I felt like "chopped liver"—that the dogs with their flat little faces and upturned chins were the main attraction.

Each of my dogs has a unique personality that shines through in sessions. Readers will see this in the stories and case studies. I cannot recall a day when they weren't eager to go to work. My routine is to announce that it is a workday, then put on their collars, and often a scarf or a coat. To be playful, I frequently match them with what I wear. When I dress them, they run up a set of stairs and onto the bed to spare me bending, since they are low to the ground. They are eager to please by nature, as are most canines who are given love and support.

The dogs have been the recipient of numerous gifts from clients. In psychotherapy, as in life, gifts have meaning, so I routinely explore with the giver what it means to them to present the gift. More often than not, these are gifts of gratitude for the love the dogs have expressed or the support they have provided in tough times. Of course, they are also on the receiving end of many compliments. I wish I had a nickel for every time they've been told how cute they are, and it's true, but what makes them most special is the unconditional love in their hearts.

The great pleasure of a dog is that you may make a fool of yourself with him, and not only will he not scold you, but he will make a fool of himself too.

—Samuel Butler

Dr. Jerry at the office

2

AT THE OFFICE

I tell all new clients that I have the dogs before their first visit. If they are not comfortable with the idea, I will not press the matter and will leave my helpers at home or in a separate and safe space at work. Again, at a first meeting, I make sure my clients are okay with meeting the dogs. Some people are deathly afraid of dogs, and even though my crew are small and harmless, a client's fear must be respected. Hopefully, in time, they will agree to meet the dogs and begin the process of extinguishing the fear. You can't get over a fear of elevators by taking the stairs, and you won't get over a fear of dogs by avoiding contact with them.

A few clients report being allergic to dogs and allergies are no fun. Fortunately, it's never been an issue, as

Brussels Griffons are non-shedders and free of dander. So, the few who have been concerned about allergic reactions have discovered they are not reactive to the dogs. Regardless, if a client is averse to having the dogs in session for any reason, I scoop them up and remove them from the area. Always and without a challenge. I might ask my client to explore their objections to having the dogs present, but for the purpose of understanding the client's thoughts and feelings, not to get them to change their mind and allow the dogs to rejoin us.

Brussels Griffons love people and welcome visitations. Mine are no exception. It is hardwired into their brains to not be aggressive and to enjoy being touched. None of mine have shown a problem with children, but because they are an emotionally sensitive breed, I would intervene if a child's teasing crossed the line. Nor have my dogs had issues with the wheelchairs, crutches, or canes used by the elderly or infirm. The only thing I have to watch for is sacks, bags, or purses. This is because the dogs will investigate with their noses to determine if there is food inside or a doggie treat. When this happens, I say to the dogs, "Leave it!" and they back off.

My routine is to have the dogs with me when I greet clients in the waiting room. I then ask the dogs if they are ready for work. They immediately stop what they're doing and run as fast as they can, leaping up the stairs to my office on the second floor. Everyone finds these antics amusing, and perhaps we all secretly envy their enthusiasm to go to work. Dogs, like people, need a purpose, and my dogs have found theirs in service to others.

Like people, dogs can be quirky, and Dr. Jerry can be annoying in that he likes to lick toes. Go figure. In the summertime, when clients come in with open-toed shoes or sandals, he goes straight for the objects of his interest. However, with a quick "No!" or "Leave it!" he stops and will pursue something else. His respect for others' boundaries makes an impression. If only *Homo sapiens* backed off and honored boundaries as skillfully as Dr. Jerry.

For counselors or others who are considering therapy dogs as an adjunct to treatment or work responsibilities, the dogs take short potty breaks in between clients. I'll say to them, "Do you have to go potty?" If they do, they'll make a beeline from my office, run down the stairs, and wait at the front door. I open the door, and they dash down the porch stairs, do their business in the bushes, and dash back in. Being a good "doggy mommy," I clean up after them, if necessary. If there was ever an emergency, they would communicate this to me through body language, and we'd have to take a quick break.

An unscheduled potty break has the potential for disrupting a session at an inopportune moment, but it hasn't happened yet. If it did, it's all grist for the mill. I would say something to my client like, "I'm wondering how that was for you. To be interrupted at a crucial time and have to stop and restart." Or, "I imagine you had some reaction to having to stop in the middle of your story. Would you be willing to share your experience?" These spontaneous moments can yield rich material for exploration. It is crucial that the client leave with the confidence that their experience is paramount and that they felt validated in whatever reaction they had.

There is no psychiatrist in the world like a puppy licking your face.

—Ben Williams

Dr. Jerry working with the orangutan at the office

3

HOW I USE THE DOGS (SETTING THE STAGE)

I consider it important to properly introduce my dogs to clients at their first meeting. This includes names, talents, and qualities.

I introduce Jack as "Jack the rebel," as he is wont to test boundaries and present with an attitude of self-importance. He has canine ADHD and is distractible and always moving, though he has learned to settle on command so as not to be a distraction. He presents himself as clever, cunning, and street-smart. Jack loves being the baby boy and the center of attention. He is naturally competitive and always has to be first. He enjoys being in control in general, and herding in particular. He would have made a great sheep dog, but for his toy size.

Dr. Jerry has been often called Dr. Fu Manchu, Dr. Freud, an Ewok, or a Gremlin. He really does look like those characters with his beard and twinkling eyes. Most often he is called "Dr. Jerry," a name given by a client who picked up on his professionalism. He is a loving and calm animal, who is wise in his ways. A draper, he likes to lie on people's laps or next to them on the sofa while hanging his legs over the edge. Clients see him as patient, sensitive, and empathic, and I have to agree. He will be especially attentive to anyone crying or broadcasting signals they are upset or suffering. In such cases, if cleared by me, he will sit on the client's lap, or less obtrusively, position himself at their feet.

This is tricky, because as a counselor, I am always trying to provide an optimal response to my clientele. If a person needs to cry or express strong feelings, I may not want Dr. Jerry to soothe them right away, as it will detract from the healing process. The goal isn't necessarily to make them feel better, it is to help them deepen their process, build awareness, develop better coping skills, and learn to regulate their emotions. So sometimes he stays back until the time is right to console. He seems to have a knack for doing this, though I confess I don't know how. If he approaches a client too soon, at least in my opinion, and interferes with their process, I will ask him to wait, and he will. He will then stay with the client until they return to a state of equilibrium, or at least until they have collected themselves.

Jenny was a very attentive, empathic mother who bore three litters. Dr. Jerry is her son. She passed away in 2011. She was very delicate, but at the same time, she could show protective qualities regarding taking care of clients and the other two dogs.

Jenny had an uncanny ability to sense when a client had been molested or abused. So accurate was she that she served as an informal diagnostic tool with clients. I recall one client whom Jenny diagnosed as having been abused in some way—she stuck by the woman's side and gazed into her eyes as if to say, "I know your pain"—but who steadfastly denied any abuse. After several denials, I said, "How were you disciplined as a child?" Nonchalantly, my client said, "I was hit with a cane." When I inquired as to why she had repeatedly denied being abused, she said, "Everyone in my culture is hit with something." (She was Puerto Rican.) In her mind, that normalized the behavior. If not for Jenny, I would have accepted what I'd been told, and this woman would have never been able to acknowledge and work through the trauma of being hit by and terrified of her tyrannical father and left unprotected by her passive mother.

Setting the stage once introductions have been made can lead to interesting findings. I brought Dr. Jerry and Jack into a couple's session (sometimes it's one dog, sometimes two, sometimes all three, in accordance with my gut sense of what will work best) with an unexpected result. This particular couple, John and Mary, had problems communicating and flat out refused to negotiate with each other. They both attended Alcoholics Anonymous, but seemed to be at a "dry drunk" stage; that is, they were sober but still acting as though they were drinking. John and Mary were alike—they had strong personalities with a desire to rebel and control. The differences in Jerry and Jack amused them, but in the end instructed them.

A typical argument between John and Mary concerned who was right and who was wrong, and both believed they had the ultimate take on reality. They were totally intolerant of differences. For instance, John would say Mary spent too much money and put them in a financial hole. Mary would say John was too tight with money; they worked hard and were entitled to spend some and enjoy themselves. They could never agree on expenditures, and each tried to make the other wrong without really listening to the other's point of view.

John and Mary watched with fascination as Jack attempted to move Dr. Jerry aside and hog the attention. Jack also resorted to trickery to take over the dog bed in the office. Dr. Jerry knew Jack was distractible and would wait for him to pursue some "shiny object" such as a ball, a chew bone, or attention from someone in the room. This would create an open space in the bed, the prime real estate, and Dr. Jerry would promptly claim it. On one occasion, Dr. Jerry led Jack over to one of the clients and while Jack received attention, Dr. Jerry slipped into the bed. Then Jack went over to the bed and climbed in with Dr. Jerry so they could share the bed.

Whereas Jack and Dr. Jerry competed for attention and the best spot in the bed, John and Mary competed for whose point of view would reign. What they learned from the dogs was that they could be so different and still get along if they communicated and negotiated more effectively. For instance, instead of focusing on who was right and who was wrong, they could clearly communicate, "I see it differently than you do." This was especially effective when both John and Mary would make a legitimate effort to understand the other's perspective—even if they disagreed with it! Now John could hear that Mary wanted to spend money so they could have fun together and that her intention was to improve the marriage. Mary could hear that John, as the primary wage earner, was concerned that financial stress would undermine their marriage, and he wanted to stay together and prosper. They could allow their differences to stand.

One session, an argument ensued over whether a joke John made was funny. It was dark humor, and Mary thought it was not funny and inappropriate. I asked, "Can you at least be curious about his way of seeing it? Isn't it okay to see it differently and agree that you each have a different sense of humor?" Using the dogs as an example, I was able to show them that there is no absolute reality that makes one of them right and one wrong, just as there is no one bed for the dogs to fight over. If Jack and Dr. Jerry can find wiser, more patient parts of themselves to share a bed, then John and Mary can do the same to share their lives without insisting they have the only correct take on reality. If there's room in the bed for both dogs, even though they are so different, then there's room in their marriage for both John and Mary's ways of seeing things.

Mary learned to say, "I don't think that's funny," rather than "That's not funny!" It may seem an insignificant change, but it's not. Saying "That's not funny!" is a pronouncement of fact, when in reality, humor is subjective; some will laugh and others not. The new way of saying it avoided arguments, as it's hard to argue with "*I* don't think that's funny." John might disagree, but he realized there was no point in trying to convince Mary she was wrong.

After several sessions of watching Jack and Dr. Jerry's antics, I asked John and Mary what made it possible for the dogs to get along so well, even though one was a rebel, and one was a sensitive good citizen. They agreed it was because Jack could let go of his need to win, and Dr. Jerry could make space for his partner. At this point, John and Mary got it. They began to learn new skills they could practice at home, using a more adult part of themselves. Both stepped back from their need to be in control and shifted into a wiser part of themselves, a part that could allow for differences.

A dog is the only thing on earth that loves you more than he loves himself.

—Josh Billings

Karen, Dr. Jerry, and Jack

4

A SECOND OPINION

All three therapy dogs have demonstrated the same amazing ability to resonate to therapeutic dialogue in sessions. Namely, they use a sudden loud snort or guttural grunt to support an idea or underline an important aspect of a therapy session. It doesn't seem to matter if they are fully awake or sound asleep. They could be in their dog bed or sitting in the lap of a client. They might be lying on their stomach, curled with a paw over their nose or sleeping belly-up.

The other day I said to a young woman client, "There's a pattern here. You keep picking boyfriends who are emotionally unavailable and then feel frustrated when they don't validate your feelings. It's like trying to get milk in a hardware store." Immediately, Dr. Jerry awakened from a deep sleep and snorted loudly. My client said, "Dr. Jerry agrees, so I guess it's so."

I don't pretend to know how they do this or what is going on in terms of brain activity. My best guess is that the dogs respond to the energy in the room and when some threshold is reached, they resonate. This could be explained by the phenomenon of the mirror neuron. This, in nontechnical language, is a nerve cell that fires and responds in the same way whether we perform an action or observe someone else doing the same action. Humans and monkeys do it all the time. Suppose you're at a softball game and you see someone smacked in the eye by the ball. You immediately wince and "read" and "feel" for the person injured. Dogs, I suspect, do the same thing—and why not? Their mammal brains also have mirror neurons.

In planning for this book, I discussed this canine resonating ability with my editor, Stan Wilson. He is a psychologist who takes his French Bulldog, Batman, to work. Batman is not a certified therapy dog but is therapeutic and much loved by his clients. Frenchies are known to be sensitive, but Stan reported he hadn't noticed Batman resonating in the way I described. Later that day I received an amusing voice mail. Two hours after I left his office a woman came for her session with Stan. Batman slept in his bed as the woman began discussing her fear of developing laryngitis and the need to conserve her voice at work. As if on cue, he awakened and cleared his throat in a really dynamic and authoritative fashion. Stan said he and his client both laughed and agreed that Batman wished to underscore what she had said. They then developed the idea of a word count for the woman, much like a pitch count in baseball (starting pitchers are often removed from the game when they reach one hundred pitches).

No matter what the reason is for these timely snorts and guttural noises, they serve to highlight the importance of certain comments or emphasize something going on in the room. When it happens, I always take the opportunity to say something like, "Dr. Jerry thinks this is important, too," or "Jack wants you to pay more attention to this," or "Jenny is giving us a second opinion." A few clients have dismissed the noises as coincidence, but most recognize that it's some uncanny message they should seriously consider.

Marilyn scheduled an urgent session regarding a bad breakup with her boyfriend. To say the least, he did not accept her rejection and had begun stalking her. This included numerous unwanted e-mails, as well as driving by her workplace and home. We worked on a safety plan that would minimize her contact with him and provide her an escape route if she needed one. We were assessing risk and the importance of safety. This she agreed to, but when I mentioned the possibility of a restraining order, she scoffed at the idea. So I called her attention to the fact that the ex-boyfriend's behavior was jealous, possessive, and alarming—she had better take it seriously. At that moment, Dr. Jerry, who'd been silent the entire session, let out a loud guttural noise to underline the importance of my viewpoint. I said to my client, "Apparently, he agrees with me." My client chuckled and came to her senses, saying, "Yeah, his behavior is pretty out of control, so I better take it seriously."

Tom came in at a time when his life was in crisis. He wanted to learn coping skills and get things in order. I suspected substance abuse from his appearance and asked a few nosy questions about his history. He denied being an alcoholic, but admitted that he occasionally drove intoxicated, had a DUI, had missed work because of hangovers, and had relationship problems because of his drinking. I didn't want to argue with Tom, so I said, "Okay, maybe you're not an alcoholic, but would you admit that you have problems with alcohol?" He agreed, so I told him that if he wanted to grow and move forward, he needed to stop drinking.

If he couldn't stop drinking on his own, I strongly recommended that he get either inpatient or outpatient treatment. At that moment, Jack, who was lying quietly and belly-up on Tom's lap, let out a guttural resonant noise to back me up. It was the first peep Jack had made in the session. I said, "Jack thinks so, too. He's worried about your health and happiness." Tom, a hard-ass guy, let out a belly laugh and agreed to take it under advisement.

Sue suffered from crippling depression, anxiety and posttraumatic stress disorder. In our initial session, without the dogs (not a policy, it just worked out that way), Sue found it hard to open up and share her story. She acknowledged a traumatic childhood but gave no particulars. She seemed quite defended, as if she would be too vulnerable to disclose what had happened. I thought Jenny would be helpful for her to feel more comfortable and brought her in with Sue's consent. Immediately, Jenny climbed out of her bed and jumped up next to Sue. She would never do that at home, only in the office when working, apparently sensing the need to support a person downshifting into talking about intense and painful experiences. I asked Sue if she was okay with Jenny next to her, and

Sue confirmed that it was. I didn't really need to ask, as Sue's body language indicated her consent, but it seemed respectful to inquire just to make certain. I have noticed a few clients, not dog lovers, who will pretend to be okay with the dogs when, in fact, they're not so sure. I wanted to be certain Sue wasn't placating me in allowing Jenny up close and personal.

With Jenny at her side, Sue began to tell her story, a harrowing tale of incest and emotional pain. She came from a very large Catholic family and suffered molestation at the hands of her father and older brothers. Her mother failed to protect her, and Sue felt completely objectified, as if she was just a "thing" for the sexual pleasure of male family members. Like many victims, she internalized shame and reported feeling dirty, ugly, defective, and alone. At times during the telling, Sue would falter and appear as though she could not continue, but then she'd take a moment, pet Jenny, collect herself, and go on. At one poignant moment, when Sue got in touch with her anger, she said, "I deserved to be protected!" Jenny, sensing the change in Sue's energy or voice tone or whatever, placed a paw on Sue and emitted a deep guttural noise as if to say, "I feel your pain."

I told Sue, "I'm honored to hear your story. When you said you deserved to be protected I felt like pumping my fist and saying, 'Yes!' but Jenny beat me to it." Sue smiled, feeling supported by two "women," and asked if Jenny could be present at all her sessions. I made a corny joke about an extra fee for Jenny, but added that she and Jenny made a good match and I would be happy to bring her along.

Sue remained in therapy for a number of years, tackling bouts of depression, addiction issues, panic attacks, and low self-esteem. We also addressed her trust issues with men (at this juncture we also brought in Jack, who embodies male energy) and expectations of exploitation and betrayal. Throughout the course of therapy, Sue bravely confronted her grief and her emotional injuries, always giving credit to Jenny and Jack for supporting her and making the work possible. Resolving trauma is difficult, but her connection to the dogs made it significantly easier and faster.

I sometimes look into the face of my dog, Stan, and see a wistful sadness and existential angst, when all he is doing is slowly scanning the ceiling for flies.

—Merrill Markoe

Dr. Jerry and Jack not quite sharing the dog bed

5

HUMOR IS THE BEST MEDICINE

❀ ❀ ❀

Sometimes a client feels so hopeless or helpless or exhausted by grief that all they have left is their sense of humor. In such instances, humor is used as a defense mechanism, a way of reducing the intensity of their sadness or circumstances. My therapy dogs are natural-born clowns. They look funny, act funny, and know how to play to the house. By making my clients laugh even while enduring the tough times, these wonderful, caring little jokers help lighten the load of life. A few examples will demonstrate their innate gift for humor.

A family consisting of both parents and two adult children came for help after a number of intense disagreements that threatened to tear them apart. I had informed them that Dr. Jerry would attend the first session, and no one objected. There was so much tension and hostility and dysfunctional communication that not much was accomplished at this initial meeting. In taking the history it became obvious that everyone blamed everyone else for the family problems, and no one would acknowledge his or her part. Dr. Jerry was quite unobtrusive; I believe he picked up on the tension and shied away. This was good, I thought, as we needed to get the cards on the table and see what the family was already doing, knowing that their current actions and relational styles absolutely did not work for them.

At the next meeting I brought Dr. Jerry again, but also Jack. I told them at the outset, "This is going to be a two-dog meeting!" and got a few chuckles. I then introduced Jack and mentioned that he likes to mix it up and would not be intimidated by the family arguments. The family then launched into their pattern of attack-counterattack and criticize-defend. Most of their complaints had to do with how they treated one another. This was always done in loud voices. "You're abusive!" "You're insolent and disrespectful!" "You're an ungrateful, spoiled brat!" "You're a manipulator!" "No I'm not. You are!" I could feel my blood pressure rising, and I was only observing.

I pushed the "pause" button (I pretend to have one on the arm of my chair) and jumped in. I asked each of them to stop with the "you" messages and to instead start sentences with "I." In other words, for Dad to stop telling Daughter about Daughter, but rather for Dad to tell Daughter about Dad. And so on. They ignored me. They were either unable or unwilling to own their feelings and clearly preferred to tell each other how they should and shouldn't be. Things got worse.

At one point, the angry daughter told her father he was a control freak and should learn to let go. I told her I had a judgment about her—that she was like an Oregon cop in Washington, out of her jurisdiction. Jack, as if on cue, barked his approval of what I said, and everyone laughed. With less tension in the room, the daughter was able to say she resented it when her father tried to dictate her choices or actions, a much more authentic and effective form of communication. When she was done, Dr. Jerry and Jack double-teamed her with simultaneous snorts of approval. I pointed out that the dogs, like me, preferred this new and different way of communicating.

It was a breakthrough that interrupted an old story in the family; namely, a blame game that left everyone frustrated and feeling inadequate. The new story of showing up authentically and owning one's position paved the way for real changes. This session heralded a new way of interacting, and the family made steady gains toward their stated goals of better communication and more harmony.

Marie had been out of work for almost three years and wept openly about her employment situation. She felt negative about her skill-sets (she worked as a book-keeper), negative about her prospects, and negative about the state of the economy. When I explained I use therapy dogs as an adjunct to treatment, she brightened momentarily and requested that I bring one. I chose Jack, as I thought he might help her to feel less depressed and hopeless. It was obvious Marie was a dog lover, and she and Jack bonded quickly at their initial meeting.

Near the end of the first session with Jack present, I asked him to do his bunny-boy trick and to give Marie a high five. Jack sat up in the chair, positioned his paws up like a bunny rabbit and did a solo high five with one of his paws. Marie let out a roar of laughter. I had never seen her smile, much less laugh heartily, so I commented on that. This led to a discussion about how she might take better care of herself by bringing some laughter and joy into her life. Marie acknowl-edged she'd allowed her depression to consume her, but that she would resume some of the activities that she'd enjoyed while employed. The session ended on a positive note.

At the next session Marie reported that she'd rejoined her hot yoga class and started again to do thousand-piece puzzles at night. She credited Jack's playfulness for helping to get her out of her nega-tivity and back into the flow of life. She said she felt more optimistic and sent out many job applications. Within a month she found a job. Whether this was coincidence or the law of attraction I cannot say, but meeting Jack certainly helped her shake her depression and negativity.

Not infrequently, Jack and Dr. Jerry fall asleep and snore rather loudly, given their diminutive bodies. If there's an opportune moment to inquire without interrupting something important, I will ask clients if the snoring bothers them. One client complained that the sound did distract her, so I positioned the boys in a way that they would be quiet. A discussion ensued about how easily irritated this client was, and she compared herself to the princess in "The Princess and the Pea" by Hans Christian Andersen.

In this fairy tale, a prince wanted to find a princess to marry but was unsuccessful. One night, a young woman claiming to be a princess sought shelter at the prince's castle. Since princesses are believed to be highly sensitive, the prince's mother devised a test. She placed a pea in the bed of the alleged princess and covered it with twenty mattresses and twenty feather beds. In the morning, the young woman complained of a sleepless night. Something hard in the bed disturbed and even bruised her. She went on to marry the prince, and the pea was displayed in the royal museum.

My sensitive client and I were able to utilize her reaction to the dogs' snoring in a way that led to several pieces of work on managing her sensitivity. Our goal was that she that would keep the best part of it (she was tuned in, empathic, and compassionate), but allow her to let go of the bothersome side (being thin-skinned, overly reactive to stressors, overidentifying with the suffering of others). Now when the boys snore, she doesn't even seem to notice, unless to make a joke about no longer being the princess.

This was the only time I recall a client objecting to the dogs' snoring. Invariably, they say it doesn't bother them and often add that they find it homey, comforting, and even funny. And then they laugh, as apparently there is something amusing about snoring (assuming one is not trying to sleep through it). I make a conscious effort to create a safe space for clients, as counseling and psychotherapy are inherently anxiety-provoking. I believe therapy dogs can play a key part in effecting this strategy.

Typically I start sessions by inquiring what my client wants to get from our meeting, or if there is a particular topic they'd like to work on. I assume clients want something or they wouldn't be in treatment, but I don't presume to know what it is from week to week. It's a little like follow the leader, and my client is the leader in initiating topics for discussion. Assuming their desire is something I can support (I can't always; for instance, a current client who is anorexic wants me to support further weight loss), I will quickly assess how the dogs might be useful. I will then run this by my client and get their agreement (or not) before proceeding. I never push the dogs on anyone, and often the dogs just sleep through an entire session without becoming involved. Their very presence is soothing.

At the end of a session, I sometimes give clients treats to give to the dogs, either as a reward for work well done or just because clients enjoy the interaction. The dogs are trained to do tricks such as sit, rollover, army crawl, bunny boy, high five, and dance. The clients get a laugh out of this, and it's sometimes a good way to end a session, especially if my client needs to reorient after doing emotionally challenging work.

I don't like to start a session with treats or tricks or humor. It changes how the session will go, and we might accidentally put the lid on something that needs to be addressed. Getting clients to laugh can reduce tension and make the work easier, but at the wrong time, it could also support their avoidance strategies. While I'd like to think the dogs have some awareness of this, I take responsibility for determining if and when they get to be entertaining and funny. In other words, humor is good medicine in therapy, but how it is timed is crucial.

A dog is one of the remaining reasons why some people can be persuaded to go for a walk.

—O. A. Battista

A joyful Dr. Jerry

6

GOING FOR A WALK

When clients become depressed, they often isolate themselves and avoid activities such as visiting friends, showering regularly, completing chores, and going to work. I've had any number of depressed and anxious clients who couldn't seem to get out of the house or refused to exercise, even if they'd enjoyed it previously. When you're down, it's really hard to motivate yourself to do what you need to do. This tends to either maintain or worsen their symptoms of depression, such as low mood, low energy, low sexual drive, loss of self-esteem, loss of interest in usually pleasurable activities, and sleep difficulties.

Valerie was a woman in her late forties who slipped into a depression after breaking up with a boyfriend.

This came after she read a Maya Angelou quote and realized it applied to her: "Never make someone a priority when all you are to them is an option." While this is sage advice, Valerie had trouble dealing with her loneliness after jettisoning the guy and proceeded to put her life on hold. Her main coping device was consuming anything with sugar, an attempt to soothe her sad and distraught self. She wisely tracked her sugar consumption and found she had spent nearly $600 on desserts at a local bakery. In one month!

Dr. Jerry sat in on my initial session with Valerie, and she was so instantly enamored she decided to get her own dog. Since I didn't know her and thought this seemed a bit impulsive, I asked her to do some research. I didn't want to be controlling, but did want to slow her down. This research included reading a book I like, *The Right Dog for You: Choosing a Breed that Matches Your Personality, Family, and Lifestyle* by Dr. Daniel F. Tortora.

I also wanted to be sure Valerie would be able to handle the cost of pet food and the inevitable veterinary bills. I encouraged her to spend some time with the dog she considered buying before permanently taking it home. Lots of pets get returned when owners realize they weren't ready for the responsibility and expense. This is not only sad, but unfair, stressful and confusing for the hopeful animal.

To her credit, Valerie did her homework and ended up choosing a cute little Poodle mix from a local animal shelter. She named him Scuppers. A responsibility she gladly accepted was to walk Scuppers several times daily. As she had a sedentary desk job, the regular walks not only gave Valerie some much-needed exercise, but she met a woman walking her dog, and they became good friends. Now they walk together, which feels safer for both of them and makes it more fun on rainy Pacific Northwest days.

On several occasions Valerie brought Scuppers to sessions to show him off, and we both laughed at the interactions between my dogs and her's. A conversation developed in which it became clear that Scuppers not only inspired Valerie, but gave her hope for the future. Of course, he provided companionship and joy, but I think what mattered most, was that he got her going and doing things, reinvesting her time and energy in activities she enjoyed. Talk about a cost-effective treatment for depression! And no side effects!

Another client, a young woman named Katie who suffers from severe shyness and low self-esteem, fell instantly in love with Jenny. I could easily see Katie's gentleness and ability to connect with Jenny and assumed it would extrapolate to other pets. At my suggestion, she now volunteers at local "no kill" animal shelters. She has such a knack with animals that one shelter allows her to take home some of the sickest dogs and cats and nurse them back to health. As you'd guess, Katie is softhearted and now has four dogs and four cats, but this is good for her. Word got around that she was a sort of "dog whisperer," and now she dog sits for families who are out of town. She even started a pet-sitting and pet-walking business, which has seen her self-confidence soar. Now Katie is considering going to grooming school, something she'd never have considered before attaching to Jenny and finding her niche. Therapy dogs are therapeutic!

There is nothing so nurturing than to snuggle with your dog. To take a nap with your dog. Especially when the dog's snore lulls you to sleep.

—Unknown

Dr. Jerry and Jack taking a break

7

DOWNTIME

While my therapy dogs like to come to work, it is still work for them. They pay attention, expend energy, and absorb energy from clients who are stressed out and most often troubled. I have no doubt that the dogs pick up on and take in clients' emotions, in particular, grief, anxiety, anger, and joy. That they take in joy doesn't worry me, but the more negative emotions need to be released.

For this reason, rest and play become even more important for therapy dogs than for household dogs. Like human therapists, the dogs need to shed negative energy from clients when they get home. I feel fortunate to live on a farm in the country, as this allows me to let the dogs run off the leash, at least when I'm with them. My rural area has many predators, including bobcats, cougars, bears, coyotes, and other wild animals who would find a Brussels Griffon a tasty morsel. I walk them around the barnyard, on makeshift trails through the woods, and by our stream. This makes them happy, and I can more or less feel them letting go of accumulated stresses from work.

Inside the house, they have lots of toys to play with and chewbones, as well. Of course, they have staked out certain areas for sleeping, something they do a lot of. In order to function properly as therapy dogs, they need more sleep than most dogs. Without enough sleep, my four-legged assistants become cranky and irritable (just like humans). I guess they need about twelve hours sleep on a leisure day and fourteen hours on a workday. It's my job to make sure they get enough.

Jack is a natural-born herder. He enjoys herding just about anything on the farm that moves. He plays regular games with the geese and the goats. His favorite activity is to taunt them through the chicken-wire fence. He starts it by barking and running, which causes the geese and the goats to try to bite or butt him. Rascal that he is, Jack is quite skilled at staying just out of their reach, thanks to the fence. He finds teasing farm animals to be great fun, and I view it as a way of relieving his work stress.

Dr. Jerry and Pinky, our pot-bellied pig, forged a strong attachment. They enjoyed touching noses and sniffed each other as if they were two dogs. Pinky's tail wagged in earnest whenever she saw Dr. Jerry at the end of a workday. After greeting each other, they would romp around the pasture and make noises at one another. It appeared to be a way for Jerry to blow off steam after a day of providing therapy.

Sometimes I would walk Pinky and Dr. Jerry on leashes together. Their favorite walk was on the Centennial Trail, a local trail off the farm, where they came to know and share familiar smells and sights. The two were best friends for eleven years until Pinky's passing. Dr. Jerry grieved intensely for his lost friend and would look for her in the places they usually met. He went through a depression and would hang his head after Pinky departed. Without doubt he missed being in her company, but mostly the fun, stress-relieving playtime they regularly shared.

Jenny favored a different form of stress relief following her days at the office. If the weather cooperated, she loved lying in the sun in the high grass in one of the pastures. She seemed to savor the peace and quiet and had a more harmonious way of interacting with the farm animals. Whereas Jack would taunt the chickens, Jenny would casually sniff them in a way they didn't mind. She might take an adventurous walk by the stream but would leave the rough stuff to the boys. Clearly, Jenny found her relaxation in a more mental and less physical way than Dr. Jerry and Jack.

Because they work as therapy assistants, I spoil the dogs at home. They get 100 percent human-grade pet food that meets the same quality standards as the food I feed my husband, my daughter, and myself. They all are given access to the highest quality veterinary medicine, kept up on all inoculations, and are taken to the vet in a timely way whenever ill or injured. In other words, I treat my dogs as members of the family. I wish every pet owner would share this commitment to their animals.

The dogs sleep either on or in the bed with me and my husband. Here, we wrestle with them, play hide the toy, or fetch. They are allowed to have chew toys on the bed, as chewing is another canine stress reliever that is wired into their brains. I like to take the dogs to the pet store and let them pick out their own toys (they favor the ones that make the highest-pitched squeaks). At the pet store, Dr. Jerry likes to bark at the stuffed animals. He finds it great fun to announce his presence to the stuffed dogs, bears, monkeys, and cats.

Speaking of the family bed, at some point in time, the dogs learned to line up, on their backs, for me to rub their bellies. This is attention they love, and it relieves stress much in the way massage does for humans. The only problem is that I only have two hands. As with humans, massage reduces doggie muscle tension, lowers their blood pressure, and reduces their stress levels. The Internet has a lot of information on how to give your dog a therapeutic massage, which only takes a few minutes a day.

In consideration of their small stature, I had two long padded window seats built and placed dog beds on them. From these vantage points, they enjoy watching the barnyard and the animals. If something takes place out of the ordinary, they bark in order to let me know. They can also see the driveway, which allows them to serve as watchdogs, a role they take very seriously (yes, there's a difference between a watchdog and a guard dog).

Until she moved from our area, I would take the dogs to the breeder's home so they could play with their siblings and cousins. This was especially stress-relieving during those times one or more of them seemed wound up. I also take them to several stores as they love to ride in the child's seat of the store carts. They often go with me to the dentist, hairdresser, massage therapist, and chiropractor. If I think one of them needs extra attention, they will sit in a chair or on the table with me. When necessary, they get professional massages and chiropractic adjustments. While this might sound silly to some, it has been an effective treatment that leads to symptom removal such as muscle injuries or arthritic pain.

The dogs almost always accompany me to my editor's office, usually one or two at a time. Dr. Jerry, in particular, knows the names of persons and places I am taking him to. He knows landmarks, apparently, and gets excited about a mile away to let me know we are near. Wherever we go, they are quiet and sit or stay on command. Knowing what is expected of them takes the stress out of most situations.

From time to time, the dogs traveled to Seattle University with me and attended classes. They would sit quietly with me, and both professors and students enjoyed their presence. Mostly they were unobtrusive, except for occasional bouts of snoring. This would typically inspire a student to make a crack to the professor about a boring lecture. While attending a class may not sound like downtime, dogs have an amazing capacity to make almost any situation relaxing—a skill all of us could use.

The dogs have had extensive training classes and also private lessons at the farm. This was a valuable and enjoyable experience for them (for me, too). We had to pass tests on an obstacle and command course in order to be certified as a therapy dog. Looking back on the training and testing, I think it is as much for the humans as for the dogs. Our dogs need us to be knowledgeable and to take the lead. Training classes also gave the dogs an opportunity to socialize with other people and their dogs. A well-trained dog is a happy, less stressed dog. Then, when the workday is done, when downtime arrives, the dogs are in a position to make the most of it.

When an eighty-five-pound mammal licks your tears away
then tries to sit on your lap, it's hard to feel sad.

—Kristan Higgins

His ears were often the first thing to catch my tears.

—Elizabeth Barrett Browning

Sad Jack

8

THE DOGS' SENSE OF GRIEF

Grief is a natural response to loss, but it is complicated, especially when we are strongly attached to the person lost. Grief is the emotional suffering, the intense anguish we experience when something crucial has been taken away. I mentioned the loss of loved ones, but grief can also be triggered by the loss of a pet, loss of health, a miscarriage, a divorce or breakup, graduation from high school or college, loss of a job or financial security, loss of a friendship, or losing a cherished a way of life when one has to sell a home or move away from what is known and secure.

Coping successfully with grief is one of life's greatest challenges and, as such, it takes time. Because everyone grieves differently, there is no "normal" timetable for processing it through. Rather, it depends on your personality, the nature of the loss, your spiritual philosophy, and the way you cope under stress. Some people say there are stages of grief, but they don't always happen, and when they do, they don't necessarily follow the same predictable sequence. The best advice is to let your feelings be, honor rather than avoid them, and get as much support as you need from others.

This is where my wonderful therapy dogs come in. All three know when a client is grieving and that it is time to go into support mode. Jenny's way would be to be extra attentive, assuming it was welcomed, and either stay close to the person's side or jump into their lap. When I say attentive, she would spend an entire hour and not take her eyes off the client. More than one person reported that her look said, "I know your pain." Even when the session was over, she would walk them to the door and through the waiting room to the top of the stairs. There, she would bid them good-bye with a tail wag or a paw shake. She did not regularly do this for clients working through other issues.

Dr. Jerry takes a straightforward approach to grief. Like Jenny, he is an attentive listener and seems to pay particular attention to tone of voice. If a client demonstrates any symptoms of mourning, he wants to touch and lick their hands. If they're not wearing socks, he will lick their toes. If they're crying, Dr. Jerry will lap the tears from their cheeks. All these behaviors require client consent, and he will look to me for a cue that it's okay to proceed. When I know he wants to lick, I'll ask the client if it's okay, assuming we're at a place in the work that would not interrupt them. If the timing is right and the client welcomes his desire, I nod my head, and he does his thing. Several clients have said Dr. Jerry's kisses are the best therapy they've ever had.

Jack responds to grief by altering his normal pace and energy level. His default mode is moving around, exploring, being energetic, wagging his tail, and jumping. This changes if a client is in mourning. He will then shift gears, slow down, stop his clowning, and stick to the client's side. He will also grunt and make little guttural sounds to underline the client's story of grief. If I lower my voice or make it gentle, he will snort and grunt as though he's agreeing with whatever point I'm making. If the time is right and I think it will be therapeutic, I will give Jack permission to climb into a client's lap and roll over. Like Jenny and Dr. Jerry, Jack knows how to attend and has wired-in empathic abilities that support my clients who are grieving.

God's finger touched him, and he slept.
—Alfred, Lord Tennyson

Grief is like the ocean; it comes on waves ebbing and flowing. Sometimes the water is calm, and sometimes it is overwhelming. All we can do is learn to swim.
—Vicki Harrison

Sweet Jenny

9

PET LOSS

Pet loss is a special kind of grief and is often felt as intensely as the loss of a relative or friend. Many people develop special bonds with their pets and consider them family members, trusted companions, and beloved friends. Here are some popular and loved pets other than dogs and cats: guinea pigs, gerbils, hamsters, rabbits, ferrets, rats, mice, horses, pigs, goats, chickens, parrots, parakeets, snakes, turtles, lizards, and geckos. My therapy dogs help clients work through their grief for any kind of pet loss.

Sadly, there are some people who don't understand that all kinds of pets are sources of fun, comfort, and companionship, and in the case of our mammalian friends, even unconditional love. Therefore, it is neither silly nor sentimental to feel intense sadness when we lose our loyal buddies. Since the therapy dogs react to the client's feelings, they make no judgments whether someone is being overly emotional. Unlike some insensitive people, the dogs would never discount nor invalidate a client's pain.

I have a current client who has pet tarantulas and is very attached to them. To each their own. Another client told of taking her pet rats, Sammy and Sadie, to the veterinarian for chemotherapy to treat their tumors. It prolonged their lives and made them more comfortable, yet many of this client's friends told her she was ridiculous. My dogs simply gave her love.

My approach in treatment is to get my clients to acknowledge their grief and express whatever feelings are present. Grief is complicated, and sometimes it is also necessary to face anger ("Why did my pet have to die?" "Why didn't the veterinarian take X-rays until it was too late?"), or guilt ("I should have built a better fence," "I should have taken her to the vet sooner"), or anxiety ("How am I going to survive without Ginger?" "What will my cat do without the littermate who's been with her for her entire life?"). Regardless of what feelings come out in session, my therapy dogs are there for the clients. They seem especially skilled in responding to clients who reminisce or tell stories about the life and times of their pets. Without knowing why, they sense that the client is upset, and their attentiveness and affection validates whatever feelings are being expressed.

A typical pet-loss session goes like this: my client comes in and becomes tearful after reporting the loss; they usually tell the story of the loss, how it happened, why it happened; and then they share what a great companion their pet has been. Jenny and Dr. Jerry console those who cry, and when the client is willing, they will get up on his or her lap. Otherwise, they will sit alongside the grieving client. As I help the client to get all his or her feelings out and assist them in saying good-bye, the dogs stay close by to lend support.

Deborah scheduled an extra session to share that she lost her wonderful dog, Lloyd. He was a small black mixed-breed dog with a spirited attitude and a heart of gold. He loved to chase his toys and jump high in the air to catch them. Lloyd was empathetic to Deborah when she was struggling with a serious depression. Like my dogs, he would be there for her and help her get through many lonely days. Now Lloyd was gone, but Jenny sat in her lap and helped her weather the storm of sadness and loss. She gave Deborah that "I feel your pain" look I've previously mentioned. As she told stories of how she rescued Lloyd as a puppy from the pound, and all the hiking adventures they'd had in the Cascade Mountains, Jenny listened attentively and allowed herself to be petted and stroked all over her body.

With Jenny in her lap, Deborah considered getting another dog right away to help her bridge the loss. This is usually not a good idea, as it interrupts the natural process of grief. Before starting a relationship with a new pet, she needed time to come to terms with the loss of Lloyd. The intention for getting a new dog should be because you're ready to move forward, not because you want to avoid suffering by distracting yourself with an exciting new puppy. In the end, Deborah waited a year, her choice, to get a new dog and acknowledged that Lloyd could never be replaced. When she showed me some photos of her new companion, she shared how useful Jenny had been in helping her get through the saddest, bleakest hours of loss. Good job, Jenny!

If there are no dogs in heaven, then when I die, I want to go where they went.
—Will Rogers

Dogs come into our lives to teach us about love, they depart to teach us about loss. A new dog never replaces an old dog; it merely expands the heart. If you have loved many dogs, your heart is very big.
—Unknown

Jenny's loving gaze

10

JENNY LEE TAYLOR

Jenny, Dr. Jerry's mother and Jack's aunt, came into my life when she was five. After deciding not to breed or show her anymore, her breeder wanted her to have a home where she would receive more one-on-one attention. She arrived with her professional show dog name, "Why Not Pop On Over." This had been shortened to Poppy, but I changed it to Jenny, which seemed a better fit. She readily adapted to her new name and soon became a part of the counseling profession. This Brussels Griffon was born to serve, and she did so with a flair.

Jenny passed her certification for Delta Society (now Pet Partners) with flying colors. "She's an exceptionally smart girl," they informed me. I beamed with pride.

She began to bark as we were going into the building to be tested, but I told her she needed to be quiet, and that was all it took. In fact, that worked so well I went on to tell her she also needed to pass her certification test. Jenny was one of those dogs who seemed to understand English, and not just for commands that had been drilled in to her. For the test, she settled right down and achieved a 100 percent score on her first try. I was more nervous than she was.

Jenny's hair was champagne in color and fine. She had a barrel chest, and those who knew her best considered her a little seven-pound dynamo. Exuberant and confident by nature, she loved people and animals but was fearless. Despite her size (or lack of it), Jenny was the alpha dog in the therapy pack that included Dr. Jerry and Jack.

Jenny was a born peacekeeper. She played the role of the mediator in any conflict over food, treats, toys, or bed space. If the boys stepped out of line, Jenny corrected them right away. When Dr. Jerry and Jack would play too hard or fight (which always turned out to be much ado about nothing), she was right there to discipline them. Jack was always testing Dr. Jerry by grabbing his legs or beard, and Dr. Jerry would take issue as he considered himself next in the pecking order after Jenny. Rough-and-tumble was okay, but if they crossed a line into aggression, Jenny would let them know they'd gone too far by putting on a show of what she could do if necessary.

An example of Jenny's protectiveness occurred on a fine day when an enormous white Great Dane wandered onto our property. He was a nice dog, and I believe he just came up the street to say hello and play. I was walking the dogs off leash, and Jenny spotted the interloper and emitted a noise that reminded me of an angry mother bear. It was a deep, roaring sound of impressive volume and immediately got the attention of the Dane. She chased the giant down the driveway and then down the street to his own property. It was quite a display, and I interpreted it as protective of Dr. Jerry and Jack. Undeterred, the Great Dane tried it again several weeks later, and Jenny put on the same performance, broadcasting the deep roar and then running after the dog until he returned home. He never came back. Those were the only two occasions I ever heard Jenny make that sound.

Incidents like the Great Dane caper showcased that Jenny was the leader of the pack, or alpha dog, on our farm. At least until the day she squared off with Annie, our Rottweiler/black Lab mix, who was six times her size. Jenny planted her feet on the pathway and stared Annie down as if to say, "You will not pass. I'm the boss around here!" Annie gazed at Jenny for a second and stepped over this seven-pound gatekeeper as if she weren't there. Jenny stood there dumbfounded and a bit embarrassed. She never challenged Annie again, and fortunately the two got along well.

Jenny's greatest gift as a therapy dog was her afore-mentioned and uncanny ability to know which of my clients had been abused. The ones who had suffered trauma were special to her, and she stuck to them like glue. She would also fix them with a loving gaze that seemed to say, "I understand, and know your pain. I'm here for you." Indeed, she was there for them, sitting close and putting a little paw on their lap at key times. When emotions got intense, she knew to back off, but when they were ready for comfort, she was right there and available.

I am honored to have worked with Jenny for approx-imately ten years. She passed at the age of fourteen and was buried with a Native American ceremony. I received over a hundred condolence cards and mes-sages from clients who remembered and valued the love and consolation she provided. May she rest in peace.

My editor, Stan, asked Dr. Dale Turner, a Yale Divin-ity School scholar, if dogs go to heaven. His immedi-ate reply: "It wouldn't be heaven without dogs!" So I'm confident our Jenny is chewing on a celestial bone or luxuriating in a field of grass.

Grieve not, nor speak of me with tears, but laugh and talk of me as if I were beside you. I loved you so—'twas Heaven here with you.

—Isla Paschal Richardson

I have sometimes thought of the final cause of dogs having such short lives, and I am quite satisfied it is in compassion to the human race; for if we suffer so much in losing a dog after an acquaintance of ten or twelve years, what would it be if they were to live double that time? The misery of keeping a dog is his dying so soon. But, to be sure, if he lived for fifty years and then died, what would become of me?

—Sir Walter Scott

Diana and Jenny relaxing on the farm

11

JENNY'S GENTLE PASSING

The decision to euthanize Jenny was a difficult one but made in her best interest, given her decreasing level of comfort and potential loss of dignity. My family and I chose an in-home passing, as we believe it is less stressful for a senior dog or, for that matter, any dog or pet. At home they don't have to deal with strangers in a waiting room and a sterile and unfamiliar environment that has been associated with fear and loss of control. A home has familiar smells and sounds and touches that make the dog feel more comfortable in his or her last moments. A veterinarian should be there to make certain the procedure goes smoothly, and to deal with any unexpected emergencies, so if your regular vet doesn't make house calls, find one who does. We were fortunate. In my area, there are a number of compassionate and skilled vets who see the wisdom in euthanizing pets at home.

Another reason for putting a dog to sleep in its own home is that other pets benefit from seeing the body. I know it was useful for Dr. Jerry and Jack to see Jenny's body at rest, as it seemed to help them come to terms with her death. Dogs are intelligent and sensitive beings who need closure just as we do. I have heard sad stories of dogs who keep searching familiar haunts for their passed mates unless they have viewed them in death. Many veterinarians think dogs are less likely to suffer as intense or prolonged a depression at the passing of a dog friend if allowed to view the body. While there may be exceptions to this rule, I believe it is most often good guidance.

That dogs understand death and grief is beautifully illustrated in the following story. Mitch and Angela and their four children had two Labrador Retrievers, Gus and Kaboom. An inseparable pair. Gus always had a tennis ball with him and always wanted to play fetch. Kaboom was more laid back. Tragically, Gus got outside the family fence one day and was killed by a car. The family planned a burial for this beloved dog, and Mitch dug a deep hole in their backyard in preparation. The family met around the burial site, and each took turns telling Gus what a good dog he'd been and how much they loved him and sharing stories of his life. Many tears were shed, and the time came to say a final good-bye. Mitch and Angela used a blanket to lower the body into the hole. At that moment,

Kaboom raced off. The family concluded it was too much for her to bear and that she'd run off, but she returned half a minute later with Gus's tennis ball. She promptly dropped it into the hole on top of Gus so that he would have his ball in the dog hereafter. Mitch placed it by his mouth. I don't think I've ever told this story to anyone who didn't at least tear up on hearing of Kaboom's thoughtfulness toward her buddy, Gus.

For Jenny's passing we performed a Native American ceremony called smudging, where we burned sacred sage and sweetgrass fanned with a feather and an evergreen branch of cedar. We also burned a special candle chosen for the occasion. Beautiful flute music played in the background. Our little Jenny gently went to sleep wrapped in a special heated blanket and cradled in my husband's loving arms. While it was heartbreaking to lose her, it was also a very tender and meaningful experience.

Coincidentally, my husband was grappling with cancer at the time of Jenny's passing and acutely aware of his own mortality. He expressed a wish that when his time came he would be accompanied by the same love and compassion that Jenny experienced. A blessing: he is currently in full remission and back to being his active self.

Quite a few clients knew Jenny well, and as she began to lose her health, they realized she was not long for the world. Toward the end, she became quite ill, as well as blind and deaf. When she could no longer stand, we made the excruciating choice to put her to sleep. For those clients who felt closest to her, I confirmed that she might be passing soon and gave them the option of expressing their gratitude and good-byes.

Some spoke to her and let her know how they'd loved her and how she'd affected them in such positive ways. Others petted Jenny lovingly, held her, comforted her, and said good-bye without words. All were appreciative of the work she did with them and the impact she'd had on their lives. I believe Jenny understood that there was a letting go with the clients who hugged her and reminded her of her many virtues. She loved the attention right up to her final breath on this earthly plane.

There is no way to do this kind of grief work without suffering, but the clients who participated in the process of saying good-bye to Jenny told me later it helped them to let go and say good-bye to their own loved ones, both people and pets. One client, Esther, came to session after Jenny's passing and reported that she repeated the same steps with her dying aunt Julie that she had used with Jenny. The experience freed her up to touch her aunt tenderly and lovingly, and to express her heartfelt appreciation for all that Aunt Julie had meant to her. She said that without having just done this with Jenny, she didn't think she could have helped her aunt pass with the same degree of skill and loving-kindness.

I received many kind and considerate condolence cards after Jenny's passing and have saved them all. To me, they reinforce the important work that each of my therapy dogs do and validated the life Jenny so enjoyed.

The soul takes flight
To the place that is invisible
And there arrives
She is sure of bliss
And forever dwells in paradise.
—Plato

My sunshine doesn't come from the skies, it comes from the
love in my dog's eyes.
—Unknown

Handsome boy, Dr. Jerry

12

DR. JERRY (JEROME SAMUEL TAYLOR)

❊ ❊ ❊

Jerry came into my life as a puppy. He weighed two pounds and fit easily in the palm of my hand. The day I brought him home I walked up to my (then) high school daughter, Katherine, with Dr. Jerry hidden behind my back. "Guess what I have?" I said. I believe she was thinking of a small, inanimate object…maybe a gift of jewelry or something tasty to eat. When I produced Dr. Jerry, she saw a tiny black puppy and commented that he was the cutest thing she'd ever seen. She jumped up and down and shrieked, "Oh my God! He's wonderful!" Little did we know just how wonderful he would become.

At birth, Dr. Jerry was a solid, glossy black, but over time he slowly shed that coat and developed a lovely red color with black accents in his beard and on his ears. His coat is smooth and hypoallergenic. The black beard has prompted clients and others to dub him Dr. Fu Manchu, an Ewok from *Star Wars*, a Gremlin, Dr. Freud, Blackbeard the Pirate, and several other characters. Sometimes Dr. Jerry serves as a walking Rorschach inkblot test.

Dr. Jerry has huge brown eyes that seem to penetrate right through to a person's soul. With this ability comes an empathetic way of relating to both people and other animals. He sincerely cares about the well-being of his fellow travelers and possesses the sensitivity and skill to put it to use. Dr. Jerry recognizes and responds to more than one hundred words. He is a no-nonsense canine who knows what's what.

At the office, he goes out to the waiting room and cheerfully greets clients, and not just mine. Many times he has claimed my colleagues' clients and refuses to leave them when summoned. It's as if he says to me, "Can't I have this brother or sister to work with, too?" He will take to their side and sit at their feet then stand stock-still and look up and smile. When spoken to, he listens attentively with an intelligent expression. Dr. Jerry, according to everyone who has met him, is a great listener. He makes deep eye contact and tips his head from side to side in response to a person's words and voice inflection.

When going for a walk, Dr. Jerry likes to take his sweet time and smell the flowers and everything else along the way. He is naturally curious, a characteristic of the Brussels Griffon breed. On more than one occasion he has nearly given me a heart attack after disappearing on our farm trails. Then, he will show up half an hour later with a look that says, "I just took a walk about, and all is well!" With eagles, hawks, coyotes, raccoons, cougars, and bears in the area, Dr. Jerry has to use good survival instincts in the woods of the Pacific Northwest. I really wish he'd never do this again, but I choose not to always tether or confine him. It goes against the boy's spirit. Recently, my husband and I moved out of the woods to a new home on the water, so I will rest more peacefully in this regard. Griffs do not like water, so he won't swim away.

At night (and during daytime naps), Dr. Jerry snores and makes guttural noises in response to his surroundings and dreams. He seems to enjoy sleeping on his back with his legs and feet straight up in the air. Needless to say, he is a clown who gets a lot of laughs. His favorite sleeping place is our bed with his body pressed up against my right side. Better yet for him is to place his head on my right shoulder and talk to me with a mixture of gentle grunts and snorts throughout the night. Lucky for me, I have an understanding husband.

As I previously explained, Dr. Jerry "speaks" with his noises in session, usually to underscore something of importance. For instance, I might say, "You're never stronger than when you ask for help," and Dr. Jerry will chime in with a snort. I might then say, "Dr. Jerry thinks so too," and then we've double-teamed the client to stop trying to do it all on their own. He also does his timely snorting in response to changes in energy. If a client gets loud and animated when talking about standing up to an intrusive mother-in-law, Dr. Jerry is likely to snort his approval. Clients universally interpret these well-timed vocalizations as supportive and welcome his participation.

Dr. Jerry loves to retrieve toys and shake them fiercely. Believe it or not, there's some wolf DNA in that seven-pound body, and it comes out when he plays like this. He will then drop the "dead" toy at my feet, or at my clients' feet, if he's in a mood to play fetch. He also likes to play hide-and-seek with his toys. If they are hidden beneath pillows or blankets, he digs in a frenzy to get to them. He has an excellent nose and never loses a toy. Because Dr. Jerry is both spoiled and curious, he feels he must sniff out any purses or sacks that clients bring into session. I typically tell him to leave it, and he does. Thank God the boy is well trained.

Over the years, clients have brought Dr. Jerry squeaky toys as gifts. One time, in his excitement, he flipped one up and struck the gift-giving client in the head. Fortunately, it was lightweight and made of cloth, and the client thought it hilarious. Most everyone finds joy in watching him play, and in this way he serves as an excellent role model.

Dr. Jerry follows a number of commands. He knows to sit, lie down, stay, army crawl, dance, rollover, leave it, retrieve toys, and roll balls. He is so smart that sometimes I just tell him what to do in regular sentences, and he discerns what is being asked of him and complies. He is a multitalented dog who knows how to relax. When at home with the other animals, Dr. Jerry lets his hair down and behaves like any other dog just hanging out. Lots of sleep and play. At work, he's all business, attending to clients for emotional cues and watching me continuously for direction. For example, he often wants to lick away a client's tears but will wait for permission from the client and me before doing so.

All of the dogs have special, matching work coats. When I get the coats out, they know that playtime is over, and it's time for work. Once we arrive in our office building, I say to Dr. Jerry, "Let's go to work." He will then do a dance and run as fast as he can, leaping up the stairs to the waiting room and my office above. Anyone witnessing this would have no doubt that Dr. Jerry enjoys his work life. I don't know what I'd do without him.

No one appreciates the very special genius of your conversation as the dog does.
—Christopher Morley

Jack the rebel

I3

JACK THE REBEL
(JACK MCCOY TAYLOR)

❀ ❀ ❀

What do you call a little dog who has to be first at everything, the hub of the wheel, the cock of the walk, who is relentlessly competitive, insanely jealous, and demands that people cater to his every whim? A canine narcissist? A doggie know-it-all? A purebred pissant? A poochie pain in the neck? This is my Jack.

Jack knows when a person or an animal is doing something they ought not be doing, and his reaction is to bark at them and call attention to their bad behavior. It's like telling on someone, and it seems to give him satisfaction. Had I known him when I was a child, I'd have disliked Jack for being a tattletale. Just try to sneak dessert before eating dinner. Or let one of our other dogs get on a piece of furniture where they're not allowed. Jack will be there to bark a protest. He tells on everyone.

My theory is that Jack dreams of being a baby until he dies. He still can't decide whether to squat or lift his leg when he piddles. Am I a puppy or a mature dog? He's the dog version of an immature Peter Pan. Like a spoiled younger brother, he doesn't want to grow up. Jack feels entitled. He wants and expects favored treatment because he is special...just ask him.

Jack's snoring can shake the ground or raise the roof. It's hard to believe a seven-pound dog can generate so many decibels. Long ago, he learned to put himself to bed at night. It's his one mature act. He's waiting when my husband and I come to bed. His head is on the pillow, and his body under the blankets. It's as if he's saying, "See, I'm human, too!" After we join him in bed, he will burrow his body as deeply as possible under the covers. It is a wonder he can breathe.

Whatever Dr. Jerry does, Jack feels compelled to copy him. If Dr. Jerry gets a toy, Jack does the same. If Dr. Jerry gets up on the bed, Jack follows. If Dr. Jerry decides to go out to play, Jack is his shadow. Dr. Jerry puts up with a lot from Jack. If I sit down and Dr. Jerry is close by, Jack will position himself between us. If both dogs are between us, Jack always has to be closest. If he isn't, he will sit on Dr. Jerry to make his point. That's right, Jack likes to sit on Dr. Jerry's head. I think this is more than merely asserting dominance. It's Jack's way of ensuring we all recognize his elevated status.

If I throw a toy for Dr. Jerry, Jack will run over and sit on the toy so Jerry can't get it. He's a buzzkill who wants to spoil Dr. Jerry's fun. He's such a prima donna he will also thwart any attempt by Dr. Jerry to get attention. It's all about Jack. If he wrote a book, it would be called *Just Jack.*

If there is such a thing as canine ADHD, I am convinced Jack has it. He is in perpetual motion except during sleep, and even then he twitches incessantly and has active and vocal running dreams. He sleeps with his eyes open, as if he might miss some action if he closed them. Jack loves to be on people's laps, but abhors any kind of restraint. Jack's motto is "Don't fence me in." Yes, ADHD is a working diagnosis!

For a little dog, Jack fills the room. A lot of dog in a small space. When I get ready for work, he practically does somersaults. He runs in a circle and pleads his case: "Take me! Take me!" This is accompanied by incessant barking. He loves work and is a perfect gentleman at the office, except for being a boundary violator. He wants to lick tears off clients' cheeks, climb on their chests, and basically be as close as he can get. I've had to train him to back off, or he would be too intrusive and interfere with the work. He obeys, but it's not his favorite thing to do.

Jack knows how to lie down, sit, come, leave it, fetch, and do the army crawl. But above all, his greatest virtue is to put aside his selfishness when I say, "Jack, where are your boundaries?" Then he will back up and sit down. The clients love it when he does this and enjoy a good laugh. Jack always comes when called and never leaves my side except when given permission to be close to the client for therapeutic purposes.

Let's just say I know why God made Jack so cute. Without his cuteness, I don't know where he would be. He is a born rebel and a boundary violator. His trainer recognized this early on and suggested utilizing his nature as part of the work with clients. That's what I've done, and Jack has become a delight to all. Rather than try to break his spirit, I let Jack be Jack. He's a rebel with a cause.

You can say any fool thing to a dog, and the dog will give you this look that says, "My God, you're RIGHT! I NEVER would've thought of that!"
—Dave Barry

Jack the rebel. And angel.

14

JACK'S SOFT UNDERSIDE

❀ ❀ ❀

Some years ago I had a client, call her Sue, who came to treatment for support of her sobriety from alcohol. Sue resisted dealing with her issues of internalized shame, as well as intense anger and anxiety. Resistance, in the sense I use it, is not a pejorative or judgmental term. It's how she survived—how she protected a vulnerable self from further harm.

That does not mean resistance doesn't get in the way of healing and recovery. For instance, Sue had learned to stuff her feelings rather than openly express them in healthy ways. She did this because it had survival value for her when she was a child. She learned early on in life that showing her feelings would make things worse for her, so she suppressed them, because it made the world a safer place. That was then. In adulthood, her resistance to healthy self-expression caused a nagging depression and a feeling of isolation and shame.

Did I mention Sue was a biker? Indeed, she came across as a very tough woman, someone you wouldn't dare mess with. I suspected there was a sensitive inner core beneath her crusty outer layer of protection. Her history included years of physical abuse by her parents and date rape as a teen. To insulate herself from an unsafe world, Sue became a rebel. This was a way of signaling her deep distrust of people and distancing herself in the interest of self-protection. While she distrusted people in general, she maintained a love of animals and knew animals loved her.

I asked Sue if she'd like to meet Jack, and she eagerly accepted. At the next session, they got acquainted. During introductions, I mentioned that Jack was a rebel and showed a lot of attitude, but that deep down he was a baby boy with a sensitive side. She smiled knowingly.

Right from the get-go, Jack took to Sue. After sniffing her, he accepted her invitation to jump in her lap and kiss her face. He was quite excited to meet this new client who clearly loved dogs, and it took him a while to settle down in her lap. After all, Jack has more than a touch of ADHD. Once he calmed down, he rolled over, belly-up, and began to snore loudly. This was unlike him to be so vulnerable and hold still on first meeting someone, and I told Sue this.

Sue began rubbing Jack's belly, which he not only tolerated, but enjoyed. She told me, "If Jack can be vulnerable and show his underside, then so can I." Then she slowly and tentatively began to talk about drinking in high school and wanting to fit in. She felt different and believed that getting drunk in a group would give her a feeling of belonging. Indeed, it worked for a while. She felt less self-conscious and made some new friends. As is often the case, alcohol worked as a social lubricant and a way to connect.

Sue's tears began to spill onto Jack's belly. As she shared her painful story, she rocked and released her pent-up feelings, all the while taking giant gulps of air. She said she attended a party where a teenage boy forced himself on her. It proved to be a horrible and traumatic experience for Sue, and she commented that she never felt the same again. Being raped left her feeling tainted, dirty, and bad - inhabiting a world that no longer felt even remotely safe. Making matters worse, she blamed herself for what happened.

After disclosing her secret (she'd never told anyone), we discussed what meaning she'd assigned to her trauma. After a long silence and a sigh, she said she believed that God found her unforgivable and unlovable. In earlier sessions, we had established her belief that God was a loving God. I asked Sue if she believed that other rape victims were beyond God's love and forgiveness, and she instantly realized the error in her thinking.

I asked her take a moment and, if she felt comfortable doing so, to ask God if she was forgiven. A few moments passed, and it seemed as though Sue was listening for an answer. She then reported that God had always loved her and that she did not need to be forgiven since she had been victimized. Getting intoxicated didn't mean she deserved to be raped. A visible sigh and tears of relief came with this realization.

Sue also gave herself credit for going into recovery with Alcoholics Anonymous and working the program. More tears of relief and release followed. It became obvious that she, not God, was the one who had withdrawn love from herself. All the while, Jack lay still in her lap. She continued to pet him, and it was clear he gave her considerable support in getting all this out.

In the process of doing the guided imagery with God, Sue realized she had been putting herself in harm's way by practicing reckless behavior with alcohol and her motorcycle. This was a bonus awareness that would lead to a lifestyle change. Even though sober, she admitted she still took chances on her bike and that this would stop. Sue felt worth protecting for the first time in her life!

About this time, Jack woke up and began to lick her salty tears. Sue did not like using Kleenex and made it clear to Jack he was welcome to attend to her crying. He enthusiastically placed both front paws on her chest and tended to her until the tears stopped. For Jack, this was a labor of love.

Sue gratefully reported that Jack helped her to get through the session. That she doubted she could have gone so deep and released so much without his support and love. She gave him her heartfelt appreciation.

This session proved a turning point in Sue's recovery. She began to reclaim her selfhood and her power, grew more confident in her abilities, and started moving on her dreams and goals. She let go of a lot of rage that she'd used for self-protection. Perhaps her most noticeable change was a newfound ability to skillfully speak up for herself. Her self-esteem improved as she expressed and accepted herself.

What Jack did was real, and it was incredibly valuable. Sue was able to set aside her resistance and go through this difficult process because she had sufficient support and nurturance. While some of this came from me, Jack played a big part. Given her belief that animals are safe and trustworthy, Jack provided the secure environment she needed to face her vulnerability. This allowed Sue to work through this particular life trauma.

It is true that whenever a person loves a dog he derives great power from it.
—Old Seneca Tribal Chief

Jack honoring boundaries

15

JACK THE BOUNDARY VIOLATOR

❋ ❋ ❋

Marianne, in her midtwenties, came to treatment dissatisfied with her job and depressed over relationships with coworkers. It soon became apparent she had difficulty speaking her mind and setting boundaries. Though she was a highly intelligent young woman with numerous work-related skill-sets, she struggled mightily with these must-have personal skills.

As a child and teen, Marianne never learned to express her feelings. As is often the case, there was an unwritten family rule not to "say what's so" to her parents. Saying what she thought, felt, needed, or wanted would lead to either disappointment or frustration, or both. She learned to not have a voice because having one and expressing herself only made things worse.

On the few occasions as a child where Marianne expressed herself, there was no one available to listen. It became emotionally easier to just shut down than to express herself when there would be no validation or payoff. Or, she would express a feeling and be either shamed or blamed. Better to shut up!

Being a woman without a voice in the workplace amplified Marianne's feelings of hopelessness and isolation. Because she was "nice," people, especially men with a need for control, took advantage of her. Niceness in a woman is often mistaken for weakness. It angered her when others took advantage or bullied her, but since she held her feelings in, it only made her depression worse. A vicious cycle.

This was hard work for Marianne, and the change didn't come easily. I explained I didn't expect her to "flip a switch" and become a master at self-assertion and boundary setting. I also called in Jack the boundary violator. I did so with her consent and explained that he could be helpful in making progress with regard to her shaky boundary setting.

I explained to Marianne that mature people respond to boundary setting by listening, honoring, and changing their behavior. Others, those with immaturity and accountability issues, don't. Such persons, regardless of how skillfully you set the limit, will continue to take runs at you. They are used to getting their way and are too insecure to admit fault or make changes.

We did an experiment using Jack. Marianne was to practice setting boundaries with him in order to see what she was actually doing. Jack climbed into her lap, and she basically had no clue how to get him to back off. He got in her face and placed his paws on her chest (all seven pounds), and she would ever so gently push, but he wouldn't get the idea. She was too passive and didn't use her voice, either.

On instruction, I asked Marianne to say, "Jack, where are your boundaries?" in a firm voice. Still she would laugh and apologize, even though Jack backed off and waited. I asked her, "Do you apologize and laugh when you set boundaries at work?" She more or less said she didn't set boundaries at work, but on the rare occasions when she did, yes, she would apologize and laugh. She said that with Jack she couldn't help it because he's so cute. But she understood that her apology and laughter undermined her power—no one would take her seriously. We practiced this several times with Jack, and I could see the light of recognition in her eyes—she truly needed to learn a more potent and grown-up way of speaking her mind.

We also practiced skill building for how to express her feelings graciously. One idea was particularly helpful to Marianne, that of self-support. We support ourselves when we stand on our center, meaning we identify what's in our immediate awareness and use it as part of our communication. She did this with Jack. For instance, "Jack, you're awfully cute, and I hate to use my strong voice to make you do things because you're so little, but you must get off me. Where are your boundaries?!" This approach worked, and she reported feeling more empowered.

The time came for Marianne to try her new skills in the workplace. She had a male coworker named Fred, not a superior, who would occasionally raise his voice or lose his temper with her. He would cite the stress he was under and offer weak apologies, but the pattern of abuse continued. Her old story was to cower in fear and say nothing about his bad behavior. Using the idea of self-support, her new story was to say something like, "Fred, when you yell at me like that, it frightens me and makes me uncomfortable. Please don't do that anymore." Notice she didn't just complain about his behavior, she translated her complaint into a direct request for change.

Marianne actually said this to Fred, and she did it without either laughing or apologizing, but it didn't work. He still raised his voice and lost his temper whenever he felt stressed out. At first, she thought this meant setting boundaries wasn't worth doing. I pointed out that it failed to affect his behavior but succeeded in allowing her to clear her register so that the unexpressed feelings didn't convert to more depression. Also, I gave her a further mini-lecture on boundaries, one that would succeed every time.

It went like this. "The problem with Fred is that he's a bully, and setting boundaries with a bully requires that you set them on your side of the dividing line between *me* and *you* (Marianne and Fred). So when you say, 'Please don't do that,' it has no impact on him for two reasons. One, he is a jerk, and two, you have no leverage. He can still do it if he wants. This means you have to set the boundary on your side. For example, 'Fred, the next time you lose your temper with me, I'm reporting it to our manager (or lodging a complaint with human resources)." Now Marianne has power, in that she can take action to produce a desired result. Notice how much more potency she has when she sets the limit on her side of the personal equation.

At the next session, Marianne announced that Fred had snapped at her in a meeting, and she told him publicly that the next time it happened she would file a complaint. He apologized. He seemed to be aware of the change in her and curtailed his bad behavior. I impressed upon her that he might test her—in fact, it was likely—and that she absolutely had to report the behavior, or she would be weaker than ever in his eyes, a paper tiger.

Now Jack is helping teach Marianne to say no. I invite him to get on her lap, and she asserts herself by saying, "No. Where are your boundaries?" He gets off her lap and sits down. Being able to say no has allowed her to stop taking on others' workloads. Her long-standing depression at work has lifted, and she credits Jack for making boundary setting a real experience rather than just cognitive talk.

The only creatures that are evolved enough to convey pure love are dogs and infants.

—Johnny Depp

Dr. Jerry practicing Jenny's magical paw on a friend, AJ

16

JENNY'S MAGICAL PAW

❋ ❋ ❋

Marissa, a delightful woman in her early sixties, came in stating her wish for a retirement filled with fun interests. The problem was that fear and guilt immobilized her. This prevented her from pursuing what she loved—photography, playing piano, traveling to exotic places, whale watching, and other outdoor activities. She felt stuck and unable to do any of it. I made a treatment plan that included parts-integration work and explained it to Marissa. She agreed this would be a good way to proceed.

Marissa suffered considerable trauma as a child. Her stepmother molested her at age eight with profound effects. She told no one because she felt bad and dirty, even though she'd done nothing wrong. As a result,

Marissa suffered from low self-esteem and social anxiety most of her life. She'd tried medication with little success, because the problem was a wound to her developing self and not a chemical imbalance.

In sharing her story, Marissa said her only friend as a child was her dog, Muffy. Except for Muffy, she felt completely alone and isolated. I would not be the first mental health professional to notice that a beloved pet is often what has allowed traumatized children to survive against all odds.

I decided to bring in Jenny, as she demonstrated a gift with adults molested as children. Jenny could be counted on to make a beeline for women and men with sexual abuse histories. How she did this I'll never know, but she would stick to their sides like glue and give them her "I understand" look. I often wondered if when Jenny was younger and not in my care, she either witnessed abuse or was herself abused.

After giving Marissa my reasons for wanting Jenny to join us and gaining her consent, I brought her in. True to form, she went directly to Marissa and sat beside her. She didn't do this with everyone, so she was either picking up on body language or an energy phenomenon, or both. Who really knows how dogs do the amazing things they do?

I cued Marissa as to how we'd proceed using guided imagery. The strategy was to have her visualize going back to the side of the bed where she was violated, but this time take her adult part and Muffy for support. We practiced what she wanted to say when she was eight but was unable to say because she was powerless and terrified of her stepmother. For additional support, she asked if she could take God along. I readily agreed.

At this point I invited Jenny to get into her office bed. She settled down next to me and expressed a few guttural noises before falling asleep. Soon, she began to snore with her eyes half-open.

Marissa began the work. After relaxing and closing her eyes, she gathered up the inner parts of herself along with her dog and her Higher Power. Now she imagined going back to the time when she had been molested. She saw her eight-year-old self and the room where the trauma took place. She stood by the bed, looked into the little girl's eyes, and said, "You are safe now. You do not have to remain here. You are no longer trapped. You can come with me and God down the road of life and let go of fear." The perverted stepmother did not show up in Marissa's imagery. Had she, I believe there would have been some choice words for her.

The eight-year-old went on to have a dialogue with God, who told her she deserved safety and did not have to remain there, that she was much loved, and that the Adult inner part and God wanted to embrace and protect her.

Marissa's closed eyes began to well up with tears. She described how the Adult inner part reached out a hand and said, "Come with me. You're safe now."

As if on cue, Jenny got up from her bed, trotted over to Marissa, and with a quick leap jumped onto the couch. Jenny nestled next to her thigh and put her paw on Marissa's hand, much to my surprise. I silently listened and watched this from across the room, not wanting to interrupt the process. I was dumbfounded. Jenny had extended her paw right after Marissa reported the image. What...does she understand English?

Marissa, eyes closed and engrossed in the imagery, reported how the inner Child had taken the Adult's hand. The Child part then climbed out of the bed, felt solid legs beneath her, and left the scene once and for all. Safe with the Adult and God, she did not have to return.

The inner parts then conversed with each other by sharing loving messages. This was reported later in the processing of this exercise. Adult and Child began to walk hand in hand down the road of life, talking, listening, asking questions, and genuinely getting to know each other.

I waited patiently until she finished and opened her eyes.

Next, we used a grounding sensory exercise that brought her fully back to the present.

Marissa looked down and saw Jenny's paw still resting on her hand. Surprised, she said to me, "Wasn't it you who touched my hand?"

"No," I replied from across the room. "I wouldn't touch you without your permission. Especially given your history. That was Jenny giving you her support."

We began to process all she had experienced, as well as what she learned. She realized that she'd been stuck all of these years in a place of fear, trepidation, and shame. She also came to realize that God had loved her all along and that the shame she felt was not reality-based, nor did it belong to her. Since she was a victim who'd done nothing wrong, there was not even a reason for God to forgive her. With a strong voice she stated her belief that she, in fact, did deserve to live a full life. It had been shame, as well as fear, that stopped her.

Speaking to the issue of using therapy dogs, Marissa said, "I'm a believer." Jenny had been magical for her. I continued to bring Jenny to our sessions until Marissa put herself out into the world doing the things she wanted to do—the things that would make her life meaningful and exciting.

I also brought Dr. Jerry and Jack to the sessions to reinforce the gains we'd made. Dr. Jerry is fearless and helped Marissa with her fear of stepping out into the world. "If this little guy can be brave, so can I," Marissa decided. Jack is the rebel who shored up her belief that she could do whatever she wanted regardless of the judgments of others.

As I write this chapter, Marissa is doing all the activities she dreamed of doing. She plays piano at her church, photographs her trips to fun places, and whale watches in different parts of the world. As if to validate her accomplishments, she posts her photos on Facebook for all to see.

She and I both give a big assist to Jenny's magical paw.

Dogs are not our whole life, but they make our lives whole.
—Roger Caras

Dr. Jerry and Jenny with my husband, Bill

17

DR. JERRY AND THE GERM FIGHTER

❋ ❋ ❋

It is quite common for people in our society to worry about germs and infectious diseases. Look at all the hand sanitizers in public places and how we're bombarded by television ads for antibacterial soaps, body washes, and household cleaners. Whereas most people don't worry excessively when they touch a doorknob or are near someone who just sneezed, people with obsessive-compulsive disorder (OCD) and a germ phobia can become consumed by fear.

My client, John, suffered from OCD. He washed his hands up to sixty times a day and took no fewer than two scalding hot showers to decontaminate himself of "germs, dirt, sweat, and bacteria." For extra protection, he took hand sanitizer with him everywhere he went, including my office. At our first session, John admitted that his fear of germs had pretty much taken over his life. His goal was to become less obsessed so he could move about the world without the constant worry.

I explained to John that OCD is a no-fault brain disorder. It appears to be related to the neurotransmitter serotonin and may be genetic. As such, we don't usually talk about cures, but clients can get much better using medication, cognitive tools, and exposure therapy. He already took meds, but they proved to be little help to John. His eyes widened when I mentioned the word "exposure." Indeed, I explained, if he kept avoiding all germs, he would never get better. As Psychologist Steve Hayes says, "If you can't have it, you will." There is a mountain of research to back this claim.

I suggested we bring in the therapy dogs. Since John didn't have a dog, I let him know that dogs don't bathe often, don't brush their teeth, like to roll in dirt, and never wipe their bottoms. John was aghast and thought I was kidding, but only for a second. My expression told him I was serious and that such an approach was a viable treatment plan. In order to heal from a germ phobia, you must stop avoiding the germs and confront the fear. Though clean, the dogs were far from sanitary and therefore were scary to John. Just what we wanted! And exactly what he needed.

John reluctantly consented. First in was Dr. Jerry, who loves to jump up on the couch where clients sit, to touch them, sit next to them, lick them (God forbid!), and snuggle. It took a while, but John eventually allowed Dr. Jerry to take a place on his lap. He even stroked Dr. Jerry to a point where he would fall asleep and snore, which made John laugh. He had successfully crossed a barrier regarding germs from animals. This gave him hope and pride.

John was slow to open up to me. He was full of shame, loneliness, and fear, and he felt like a pariah with his OCD. Gradually he began to talk about his childhood experiences, in particular being abused by his siblings. He told me about his adult life and relationship history, especially the part about going through a painful divorce. He shared his story and connected with me, all the while cuddling with Dr. Jerry.

The therapy progressed on two levels. On the first level, John allowed himself to be exposed to potential germs from Dr. Jerry, letting go of his previous avoidance strategy, which he admitted hadn't worked and never would. On the second level, we used guided imagery to work through the old issues around abuse and internalized shame. A third level involved skill building, such as learning to say no and setting limits, managing depression and anxiety, meeting new people, and trying to stretch himself regarding his dreams and goals. Because of his OCD and germ phobia, he had never learned these skills prior to treatment.

When it came to setting limits, I brought in Jack, the rebel and boundary violator. John practiced saying, "Jack, where are your boundaries?" Jack, as previously explained, would back up and sit down. As John gained a skill, he also exposed himself to another little germ factory. Working with Jack helped to generalize the gains John had made previously in his work with Dr. Jerry. He needn't like germs, but he must learn to accept them.

John started getting better. One session, I gave him a homework assignment to touch at least one public doorknob a day. He surprised himself by being able to complete the task. He reported feeling "incredibly uncomfortable," but he realized that the germs wouldn't kill him. This experience empowered John, and he became more involved in his life, rather than being holed up in his ultraclean and sanitary home.

At another session, John announced his decision to get a dog. We discussed an optimal breed, given his life-style and preferences. He ended up rescuing a small-ish Shepherd mix from the pound and named him "Purell" after the sanitizer brand. Purell helped John with his to-do list—namely, exercise more and get out and meet new people. The two took daily walks, always trying out new parks, trails, and hikes. This led to a few new friendships. The avoidance of germs and worry about contamination no longer ruled John's life.

With his germ phobia well managed, John became more engaged in his hobby of photography (which involved going out), playing the organ (even ones others had touched), joining a church (lots of hand shakers and even a few huggers), and starting a new list of goals he is presently checking off one-by-one. None of this would have been possible without his risking exposure to the dogs' germs and extinguishing the fears he associated with potential contamination. Worrying about germs no longer ran his life, and no longer ruined it. Good assist by Dr. Jerry and Jack!

If your dog doesn't like someone, you probably shouldn't either.
—Unknown

If a dog will not come to you after having looked you in the face, you should go home and examine your conscience.
—Woodrow Wilson

The attentive Dr. Jerry

18

THE CLIENT DR. JERRY DISLIKED

✤ ✤ ✤

Fortunately, it wasn't my client. I share a building and the client in question worked with another therapist. He was a young man about twenty-five years of age, dressed all in black. He stood sulking, hunched over, and seemed to emanate angry energy from every pore of his skin. No doubt the young man had a lot on his mind and, I theorized, some abuse in his history.

Dr. Jerry spotted the fellow from across the shared reception room and started to bark. He would have run over to him, but I said, "No!" Dr. Jerry stayed as commanded but emitted a low growl until I took him into my office.

My interpretation of Dr. Jerry's response was, "This person should not be in our space. He is unsafe!" On entering my office, our sanctuary, Dr. Jerry stopped growling for a moment, looked back, and let out a final growl. It was as if he was saying, "I'm telling you. I don't like that guy's vibes. He does not belong here."

An hour later, when my next session ended, Dr. Jerry asked to go out and immediately went to the spot where the young man in black had stood. He sniffed and seemed satisfied he was gone.

It should be noted that Dr. Jerry behaved this way because he felt threatened. He is usually friendly to strangers, but he wanted to communicate something about this particular fellow. He shared with me his discomfort through dogspeak. What exactly triggered this, what the dog picked up on, I do not know.

My editor, Stan Wilson, is a psychologist who takes his French Bulldog, Batman, to work with him. Stan, on discussing this chapter, told me a story about the only time Batman ever growled at a client.

Stan had a client who came for marital therapy. Stan's take on this guy was that he was uncommonly defensive. He didn't necessarily pick up on any kind of anger problem. But interestingly, the client's estranged wife had left him because, she said, "He's intensely negative, and the kids and I are tired of his angry explosions." Batman apparently picked up on this aspect of the client's being when Stan didn't.

Stan interpreted Batman's communication as, "This guy could be dangerous...I am signaling that I recognize the threat so he won't mess with me (or you)."

When the client denied his wife's assertion that he was angry or explosive (remember, he was uncommonly defensive), Stan asked what the couple's two girls would say about that if brought in. The client agreed they too would see him as having anger management problems. But that they were wrong.

Stan then pointed out that he was apparently perceived as angry and scary. Even Batman felt threatened, and that it behooved the client to look at what he was thinking, feeling, or doing that made others uncomfortable—even if he didn't see himself that way.

In subsequent sessions, the client admitted that he had a high need for control and that it infuriated him when he couldn't call the shots. He asked Stan if Batman growled at many clients, and Stan answered that he'd not only been the first, but the only one. This helped him own his problem, because Batman, unlike his wife or children, had no ax to grind. The client made a concerted effort to manage his anger more effectively, drink less alcohol, and start meditating. As of this writing, he has made considerable progress.

Your dog is your only philosopher.
—Plato

Dr. Jerry and Jack at work

19

THE YIN AND YANG OF THE OFFICE

❀ ❀ ❀

The dogs' bed is dark blue and circular. It is small, but plush and comfy. The dogs prefer to fit themselves into the bed nose to tail, perfectly filling it to capacity. They like structure and sameness, so the order never varies.

Clients love the order and the consistency of their respective positions in bed. More than one told me it reminded them of yin and yang—in Chinese philosophy the passive female and active male principles of the universe, respectively. They also say the dogs' predictability makes them feel good, more harmonious. They see the dogs enjoying their bed and enjoying one another, and this too gives them a feeling of contentment.

Yin and yang are complementary forces that manifest as dualities (sun and moon, hot and cold, light and dark, life and death). My clients typically associate yin and yang with the up and downsides of life. This leads us into meaningful discussions of their belief systems, what they stand for, what their most cherished values are, and how their religious or philosophical beliefs support them. It also generates discussions about the best and worst things that have happened to them.

Some clients observe and express their wish for closeness and warmth in a relationship. Others state a wish for the dogs' sense of safety and security, especially when they were small and vulnerable as children. Many valuable conversations have come about from noticing the bed and the dogs' relationship to sleep and to one another.

A recent client, Bud, admitted cheating on his wife. Bud is a nice man who felt trapped in a loveless marriage and "stepped out," not for sexual gratification, but for the love of another woman. He offered this not as an excuse, but as an explanation of his behavior, which he himself judged as wrong. The yin/yang discussion came about in the context of good and bad morals and whether he had gone from being a good husband to a bad one.

When Bud expressed a wish for the simple life of the dogs, I pointed out that he too could live a life of natural self-regulation, just as they do. Bud got it that the issue was not as simple as good or bad; it was about being honest about what he needed and wanted out of life and then proceeding with honesty and integrity.

He said, "I wish I could trust and be trustworthy like Dr. Jerry and Jack and Jenny." And I said, "You can." As soon as I said this, he understood.

Bud admitted the affair to his wife and filed for divorce. They had lived separate lives for years and had stopped being affectionate or intimate. He wrote a letter to his (adult) children that acknowledged his transgressions, his lies, his poor choices, and his humanness. He asked for forgiveness. A Catholic, he confessed to his parish priest. Again he referred to the dogs' simple lives and how he wished to emulate them. In the end, he did, choosing a life of responsibility and authenticity.

Dogs are better than human beings because they know but do not tell.
—Emily Dickinson

Husband, Bill, with Jenny, Jack, and Dr. Jerry

20

TRUST AND VULNERABILITY ARE VITAL (THE PLATFORM FOR THERAPY)

It's not easy to acknowledge being depressed, suffering from loss, gripped by anxiety, harmed by trauma, practicing an addiction, failing at a career, or being unable to solve a relationship problem on one's own. It means exposing a vulnerable self to criticism and risking embarrassment and shame. Yet this is what all my clients do.

The typical client comes in, discloses some very personal problems, and makes herself or himself emotionally vulnerable. Make no mistake, coming to counseling or psychotherapy is not for the faint of heart. Clients end up telling stories that require them to relive trauma and ride an emotional roller-coaster as they bare their undersides. They need to be in a place where they can speak the unspeakable, or the process won't work. Because of this, it is incumbent on me as the therapist to provide a safe space.

I have come to see how my therapy dogs help to create an atmosphere of safety, security, and trust. This happens primarily as clients observe my interactions with the dogs, how I handle them, how I care for them, and how I take an alpha role in a nurturing and humane way. My structure and rules in using the dogs also builds safety.

I introduce Dr. Jerry, Jenny and Jack as respected colleagues. The dogs trust me implicitly and are relaxed in my presence. They respond well to my requests and commands. All were clicker-trained and have been treated gently and lovingly throughout their lives. They have been disciplined, when appropriate, but never spanked or hit. They know what is expected of them and expect to be treated lovingly and consistently.

Perhaps clients see me as trustworthy because I have earned the trust of these little vulnerable and dependent animals. My dogs and I have shared a number of experiences, and they are used to my being with them in new situations or circumstances that might otherwise be stressful. They have interacted with many other dogs, an assortment of farm animals, numerous clients with many different self-presentations, scores of other people, and a variety of places.

Dr. Jerry actually flew with me in a single-engine plane from Snohomish, Washington, to Chelan, Washington, a distance of over 150 miles. The expression on his face was indescribable when he looked out and saw that we were flying over mountains. He tipped his head, and if I had to guess at his thoughts, I think he was saying, "I don't understand, but I feel safe with you."

The clients see that I treat the dogs gently and with love. I can't be certain, but I believe they expect that I will do the same with them. A few have expressed this sentiment. For instance, a young woman told me, "I see how sweet you are with Jenny, and it helps me feel safe with you…like it's just a part of who you are." Being gentle and respectful allows clients to be more vulnerable because they feel safer.

I believe I was always good at creating a safe space for my clients, but since I started working with the dogs, I realized that clients opened up more quickly and got their work done faster. I also noticed that we connected and bonded in less time than before the dogs assisted. I only wish I'd started working with the dogs sooner.

I cannot imagine working without the dogs. If I can't bring a dog to the office for some reason, coworkers and clients always ask, "Where are they?" It's clear they are expressing disappointment. "What am I," I jokingly ask, "chopped liver?" Perhaps clients feel a bit less safe when the dogs are not present for the session. Hard to say. I'll make it a point to ask if the time seems right.

Typically, the dogs greet clients in the waiting room and escort them into the office. Clients choose where they sit, and the dogs wait for cues as to whether they should sit close-by, or get in their bed. I want to be sure they're not intruding or changing the course of the session. Especially at the outset while we're searching for a focus or theme.

The first minute of every session is crucial, a time where clients will say what they want for themselves or indicate a topic for conversation. I don't want that to be about the dogs—unless it is, but that would be rare. Clients don't come for the dogs, they come for emotional relief or to make changes in their lives. Sometimes there is a minute of banter about the dogs, but this feels more like the client is getting comfortable before settling down to business.

Once we are into the meat of a session, the reason for the client to be in therapy on that day, we focus. I like to get one nail into the foundation and really hammer it down, rather than get a bunch of nails in, but only halfway. Having the dogs present settles the energy in the room and allows that important focus to take place. It also enhances the trust that makes it possible for clients to risk being vulnerable, so they can go deeper and get the most out of their therapy.

The client, the dogs, and I form a team. Our goal is to bring about greater awareness so that the client can change—if they so choose. For example, a client may be trying to decide whether to leave a verbally abusive spouse. My role isn't to get them to leave, but to get them to a place of maximum awareness so he or she can make the optimal choice.

Nearly every client presents with some difficult issues, and most report feeling safer while holding the dogs. If this facilitates a more authentic sharing of feelings as they move toward their stated goals, then I call it good teamwork.

I think dogs are the most amazing creatures; they give unconditional love. For me they are the role model for being alive.

—Gilda Radner

Dr. Jerry and Jack with friend, Karen

21

DR. JERRY AND JACK
(THE TEAM)

❋ ❋ ❋

Some years ago, I had a charming client I'll call Mike, a young man in his late teens. He came to therapy reporting problems communicating with people in general and his family in particular. Mike had a past history of trauma but also suffered from ongoing bullying in his home, inflicted by a younger brother. This brother had issues with boundary violations, throwing tantrums, and basically running the show with his family. My client felt pushed into the background by his brother's poor conduct. This was a mixed blessing. He didn't get the attention he needed but was often grateful to be off the radar so his brother would not pick on him. The parents were remiss in not holding the brother accountable, and Mike felt, understandably, unsafe.

I decided to bring Jack and Dr. Jerry into the office because their relationship is somewhat similar to that of Mike and his brother. Mike agreed to this move, especially after I mentioned that the dogs had an interesting sibling rivalry. I further explained that Dr. Jerry is easygoing like Mike, and that Jack is jealous, competitive, and attention-seeking like his bully of a brother.

Mike came in that first day with the dogs and immediately sat on the floor, not his usual place to sit. Normally he sat on the couch but chose to be on their level. Right away Mike had a laugh when Jack came over and sat on Dr. Jerry's head. If Dr. Jerry sought attention or affection from Mike, Jack got between them in a way that made touch virtually impossible.

Mike agreed: Jack was just like his brother, and he was just like Dr. Jerry. It was uncanny. I asked him for examples, and then we discussed how the relationship could change. By watching the two dogs interact, Mike developed a new perspective on his stressful family situation.

I proceeded to teach Mike how to deal with bullying, or maybe I should say Dr. Jerry did. Mike came to realize that by being so reactive to his brother, he actually encouraged him. Seeing how Dr. Jerry took it in stride inspired him to let it go (assuming he wasn't being injured). This is often the case. Bullies want attention and control and only continue if reinforced.

I also taught Mike to set effective boundaries, to carve out his own space in his own bedroom, to take time-outs away from his brother when he escalated and, above all, to develop his own life separate from his parents and brother. I explained how Dr. Jerry did all these things instinctively and that he could too. He realized he was too tied in to the family and needed to separate to develop his own identity.

Though I don't always do this, I ended up bringing Dr. Jerry and Jack to every session. Mike stated that watching the dogs helped him to cope better with his less than optimal circumstances. By becoming less reactive and better at boundary setting, he felt safe enough to open up and deepen his communication skills both in his home and out. He said that his brother picked on him much less because Mike had taken the fun out of it. He also asserted himself with his parents in a way that let them know that by not disciplining the brother, they were letting both sons down. He felt empowered saying this even if nothing changed.

I believe Mike's experience with the dogs facilitated these important changes in a way that talk psychotherapy by itself would not have accomplished. Experience and observation are the best teachers!

Petting, scratching, and cuddling a dog could be as soothing to the mind and heart as deep meditation and almost as good for the soul as prayer.
—Dean Koontz

Perhaps one central reason for loving dogs is that they take us away from this obsession with ourselves. When our thoughts start to go in circles, and we seem unable to break away, wondering what horrible event the future holds for us, the dog opens a window into the delight of the moment.
—Jeffrey M. Mason

Dr. Jerry up close and personal

22

DR. JERRY AND THE
ANXIOUS CLIENT

❋ ❋ ❋

Nancy, a middle-aged woman who had never before been in therapy, came in with the goal of dealing more effectively with anxiety. When asked, she was unable to recall a time when she did not suffer from apprehension and worry. Medication helped, but she felt understandably anxious about becoming dependent and experiencing long-term side effects. This is a valid concern, as I believe the medical community is far too cavalier about dispensing addictive medicines for anxiety. And new research suggests some anxiety medications can cause early senility.

On meeting Nancy for the first time, Dr. Jerry endeared himself by approaching her and indicating he wanted to be picked up. She asked if that was okay, and I consented. Once in her lap, Dr. Jerry settled down and listened to her as she spoke with me. She proceeded to disclose a history of childhood abuse and how it continued to affect her in terms of not just anxiety, but also depression and shame.

Dr. Jerry soon fell asleep in her lap and snored with a rhythm that seemed to relax Nancy. To my surprise, she reported that this moment was the first time she could remember feeling safe and secure. She said she loved to hear him snore and to observe him as he relaxed in her lap. At this point, Dr. Jerry had his head on her knee and draped his legs over hers. She stroked him gently and made a point of telling me how much she enjoyed his smooth coat. When he awoke, he looked into her eyes, and she commented on how sweet she found his expression. I asked Nancy to put words to the look he gave her, as if Dr. Jerry could speak. She thought he was saying, "I care about you." Whether this is true or not matters less than that it was her experience.

Over a period of several months, Nancy came to see the time with me and Dr. Jerry as a safe place to work on her trauma issues. To speak the unspeakable and not get in trouble for it was a relief. We identified a lot of automatic negative thoughts about herself and how we could dispute them or detach from them. We also spoke of reframing the way she saw the world and herself. So, for instance, instead of saying, "I am a victim," she would tell herself "I am a survivor!" And not just saying the words, but really validating herself for surviving all that she'd endured. Her story about herself gradually changed.

With awareness and intention, Nancy let go of her negative self-talk and became a better friend to herself. She learned to catch herself before putting herself down or abandoning herself during times of stress. One session, she came to the realization that she needed to relax her body, as well as her mind. Soon after, she learned to meditate, and she also joined a yoga class. As she practiced these disciplines, she realized her anxiety was dissipating and, in its place, she felt more competent and confident. Significant changes were happening, not the least of which was an ability to manage her fears and let go of her past.

Nancy started a candle collection she could burn and did so while in her bubble bath as a way to enhance relaxation. She used incense to set the mood along with music that "relaxed her soul." To cover all her bases, she attended body movement classes and attended local dancing activities. She brought effort and aim to her anxiety problem.

The emphasis on body relaxation showed in her interactions with Dr. Jerry. She became much more physically playful and would get on the floor with him to mock roughhouse. She brought him toys she could throw so he would fetch. When she brought in treats, she would tease him a little and make a game of it that even involved getting him to chase her. Needless to say, she became one of the good doctor's favorite clients, and he would run out and greet her in the waiting room with an enthusiasm that surprised even me.

As has happened with other clients, Nancy decided to get her own dog. This is an unintended but welcome by-product of working with therapy dogs and seeing what a joy they can be. Nancy adopted Jimmy – he was quite calm for a black Lab - and they took long walks together and bonded. They played together daily and snuggled on the couch at night. She had been living alone, and she also reported feeling safer with a good-sized dog in her home.

Nancy told me that Dr. Jerry taught her how to let go and relax. Now Jimmy was reaping the benefits. I believe this is accurate. Dr. Jerry even was a role model of relaxation and trust for Nancy. She committed to a list of positive activities to keep herself present and centered, therefore less prone to anxiety. She credited Dr. Jerry for her newfound sense of inner peace and even sought out a spiritual way of living her life. What a blessing for me…to see my little Dr. Jerry have such a positive influence on a nice woman who had previously been suffering.

If you don't own a dog, at least one, there is not necessarily anything wrong with you, but there may be something wrong with your life.
—Roger Caras

Jack and Dr. Jerry

23

JACK AND JILL

❋ ❋ ❋

Jill, a professional woman with a master's degree in business and an impressive résumé, came in to discuss her conflicts in preparing for retirement. To Jill, retirement meant standing still, and that meant the necessity of having to face herself and her feelings. A self-confessed workaholic, she numbed out by always being on the job and was afraid retiring would allow a flood of painful emotions.

In particular, Jill felt intense guilt and shame about the poor relationship choices she had made. Making matters worse, she believed God had not forgiven her and that she would forever be punished. On the surface, retirement would mean more time to relax and do meaningful activities, but Jill knew that with all the extra time, she would have to face her unresolved issues.

I thought Jack might be helpful and told her so. I introduced Jack to Jill and explained that Jack was a rebel. I told her that I brought him in because I sensed a rebel in her who was being thwarted. At first Jill balked, thinking of a rebel as a person who resists authority for no good reason. I gave a more positive definition—namely, someone who resisted being controlled and lived an adventurous life. She liked my definition because of her penchant for choosing controlling men who ruled over her and then avoiding them by devoting herself to the workplace.

In that first session with Jack, Jill said, "I can relate to his rebel," and wanted to embrace the one in herself. She invited Jack to join her, and he promptly got out of his bed and jumped on her lap. For the next half an hour, Jill told her story of abuse, which had started in her family-of-origin and continued into her adult relationships. Jack and I listened attentively as she poured out her feelings of hurt, grief, and anger. When she finished, I asked her to think about her rebel and how she could use that part of her to create a new way of being in the world.

Jill looked down at Jack, petted him lovingly, and said, "If this little guy can be a rebel, so can I." I asked her to make some sentences that start with, "My rebel has decided to_____." She looked at Jack as if he were a talisman with magic powers and answered, "I would use my retirement to give free rein to my creativity," "I would train to be a sculptor," "I would buy more horses and go for adventurous rides around the country," "I wouldn't give a damn what anyone says about how I'm choosing to live my life!" The written page cannot convey how Jill said these things, but I will tell you her voice was strong, confident, and decisive. A far cry from the defeated and timid woman who avoided her feelings by never slowing down.

Jack inspired Jill and helped her to find a place within herself that she had buried and never developed. With Jack in her lap, she faced her feelings and forgave herself for the bad choices she'd made along the way, realizing they had been set in motion by a history of abuse and trauma.

Jack continued to come in and join Jill as she geared up to retire, and after she retired, he was there for her as she carried out her creative and adventurous dreams. Jill's strength came from her pursuit of outdoor activities—walking, gardening, working on her farm, and riding her horses. She loved nothing more than vigorous horseback rides in the mountains, even though there was an element of danger involved. Citing her age, people warned her off, but she didn't give in to their negativity.

Without the assist from Jack, Jill would have never identified the rebel in herself and given this part its due. It allowed her to enter retirement with an attitude of excitement and creativity, of dancing to her own drum. She became more of a free spirit who chose to live life according to her own rules rather than to let men define her. Her independence and spontaneity remind me of a small canine I happen to know.

Histories are more full of examples of the fidelity of dogs than of friends.
—Alexander Pope

Daughter, Katherine, with Jack, Dr. Jerry, and Jenny

24

ALL THREE AND MEGAN E.

Megan E. was an attractive, well-educated professional woman referred by her primary care physician. She made clear to me in our first session that she came reluctantly ("I don't want my head shrunk"). Megan acknowledged struggles with depression, obesity, and sleep apnea, but she didn't see what good psychotherapy could do her. When pressed, she reported her only reason for coming was to placate her doctor and "get him off my back."

I include Megan's case here because I think it is representative of how animal-assisted therapy can be used with clients presenting with motivational or resistance issues. After clarifying with Megan that she had come under duress, I asked her if she'd be willing to attend just six sessions to see if therapy could benefit her. If she saw no benefit she could at least tell her doctor she'd tried.

Megan agreed to the time-limited six-session contract, and in the course of the discussion, she acknowledged that talking to a mental health professional was threatening. At this point I spoke briefly about my three dogs and how I use them in treatment. She softened a bit so I suggested introducing them to her at our next session. Megan consented in a neutral way.

There are generally three stages in animal-assisted therapy. Stage one is to meet privately with the client, try to understand why they are in my office, and ask them to state what it is they want from therapy. This is done without the dogs, but here I bring up the idea of using them and why. In Megan's case, she was there not of her own accord. Her "goal" was to silence her physician, who'd been encouraging her to attend therapy sessions over the course of the time he treated her. I wish all medical doctors were so aware and committed to treating the whole person!

Stage two is to introduce the dogs and hopefully begin to develop a bond between the client and the three of them. Dr. Jerry, Jack, and Jenny all attended. To encourage the bonding process, I invited Megan to give them treats and to deliver verbal commands such as sit, stay, "Watch your boundaries," etc. Megan was delighted to interact in these ways. She observed me playing with the dogs and caring for them, and I believe this helped her view me as more human and less threatening. She stated she looked forward to session three, so this in itself seemed like progress.

Stage three could take a month, a year, or longer. It includes the hard work of increasing awareness, lessening the effects of trauma, reducing the pain of symptoms, and working through grief and shame. It is time spent in the service of providing what the client wants and needs to meet his or her goals.

At the next session, our third and the beginning of stage three, Megan felt safe enough to state some goals: "Be less depressed and stop diving into the fridge for comfort food." When I shared with her that I, too, have used food as a way of soothing myself when anxious or depressed, she clearly felt more connected and less ashamed. After that, her play with the dogs was more spontaneous and joyous. She actually seemed to look forward to session four.

Session four began with an announcement. Megan had decided to get a dog and a cat as companions. As she often worked from a home office, she indicated she would walk the puppy regularly and give both pets all the attention they would need. Her mood had brightened and began to refer to my dogs as her "three babies." She asked to rescind the six-session agreement and really get to work on her underlying issues "for as long as it takes."

There was a good deal of abuse in her family-of-origin history, and Megan tackled it head on. Coming out of denial and owning her story, she realized she'd suffered a lot of trauma and that this was a cause of her lifelong depression and weight issues. For the first time, in her life, she set boundaries with those who'd abused her. She also joined Weight Watchers and committed to taking better care of herself. Megan disclosed her reason for not coming to therapy sooner was that she feared being judged or criticized, but that she felt safe to open up with me and the dogs in the room. Her resistance, which had served to protect a vulnerable self, had dissolved.

During stage three of animal-assisted therapy that we focus on achieving the client's goals and then monitor improvement. In Megan's case, this was a slam dunk! Not only did her depression lift, she also learned to eat more healthfully and limit her portion sizes, and she began an exercise program at a gym for women only ("less self-conscious"). Megan lost over one hundred pounds without surgery, and this alone eliminated her sleep apnea symptoms. Amazing! Not surprisingly, her self-esteem skyrocketed along with her energy level and zest for life.

Megan terminated therapy (or at least is taking a recess), but checks in twice a year by telephone. She continues to make gains in self-acceptance and self-confidence and feels much more compassion for herself and others who struggle with weight and body-image issues. I so admire her courage and tenacity and tell her so every time we talk. At our final session, I asked what made the difference that led to her really investing in therapy and in herself, rather than placating the doctor who referred her.

Megan answered, "I grew to feel safe in the dogs' presence. Dogs don't judge you. They don't know you let yourself go, let yourself get fat, let yourself fall into depression. Now I have my own pets...my own family. I'm not lonely anymore, and I'm really starting to love myself for the first time in my life."

My take is that this feeling of safety allowed Megan to motivate herself to work on her problems without the fear of being shamed—which is what she'd come to expect growing up in a toxic family environment. She could now be vulnerable and face her difficult history in a place of safety and security. As we worked through her traumas, she developed a better sense of belonging and a more gentle way of being with herself, a way first shown to her by Dr. Jerry, Jack, and Jenny. If only people could be so kind and compassionate, not to mention nonjudgmental and unconditionally loving.

Dogs do speak, but only to those who know how to listen.
—Orhan Pamuk

Questers of the truth, that's who dogs are; seekers after the invisible scent of another being's authentic core.
—Jeffrey M. Mason

Diana holding Jack and Bill holding Dr. Jerry

25

DR. JERRY AND COUPLES

Dr. Jerry has proven to be the best choice when I'm doing couples therapy. He is by far the best listener of the three dogs, and this pays off whether the couple comes to my office or we meet at their home. Yes, I do home visits, because seeing people in the artificial environment of an office changes things.

Working "in vivo," that is, in the couple's real living environment, gives me a chance to see them in their own surroundings. Sometimes this yields invaluable information such as when I worked with a couple and discovered the husband had a television in every room of the house, excluding bathrooms. When I asked the wife about it, she explained that they would all be set to same channel (sports). The volume would be set so loud that she could hear them when she drove into the neighborhood. I am not making this up.

Another time I learned an able-bodied "stay-at-home wife" (her term, they had no kids, she had no reason <u>not</u> to get a job), simply ignored housework and let the house be a cluttered, dirty mess. Still another time, I discovered the husband was a survivalist, with an arsenal of guns, a bomb shelter, foodstuff supplies for months, and conspiracy theories that were, frankly, bizarre. In all these situations, I would also watch Dr. Jerry's reactions to my clients' homes, as he would tag along. His comfort vs. stress level (he clings to me if the vibes are bad) was a good gauge of what was going on. Such findings might or might not emerge in regular office sessions.

Couples often come for help because they're angry at each other. Resentments have developed over time and festered; then they have turned into bitterness. Expectations of unconditional love and happiness have not been met, and they blame each other. A problem with almost every conflicted couple is that they see the world differently, but can't let the difference stand. Instead, they argue that their reality is THE ONLY REALITY and that they are RIGHT and the other WRONG. Needless to say, this only make things worse by polarizing them and creating tension.

Typically, even if he's in the room, I want Dr. Jerry to stay in his bed at first so I can get a window into what's going on with the couple. My job isn't so much to change them as to help them see their patterns, their ways of communicating and relating, and let them decide if they want to try something different. I get the couple talking to each other about their issues rather than telling me and expecting me to either referee or fix the situation or both. This is where Dr. Jerry comes in. An example will illustrate.

Tom and Mary came in very angry at each other, citing primarily a lack of support and also distrust. In our first session, without Dr. Jerry, I could see their complaints had merit. Mary would complain that Tom was unaffectionate and that she was expected to do everything. They both worked full time, but she did 90 percent of the housework and yard work. When she complained to him about the unfairness of this, and she did, she did so unskillfully. Predictably, he became defensive and invalidated her feelings.

Tom objected to Mary's Facebook relationships with old boyfriends. He felt threatened and distrustful, and she basically said it was none of his business since she was sexually faithful to him. As they talked about these issues, emotions would escalate, and nasty arguments would ensue. Loud voices, red faces, high blood pressure, bad vibes, eye rolling, stonewalling, lots of tension in the room, and blaming, with neither listening to the other. I learned I was their fourth couples therapist. I believe the others burned out.

With Tom and Mary's consent, Dr. Jerry came to the second session. I explained that he was a good listener and a lightning rod for tension (in other words, good at diverting negative energy). Sure enough, a few minutes into the session, Mary complained that Tom had agreed to load the dishwasher on a Friday and it still wasn't done (this was a Monday). He responded by saying it was no big deal, that dirty dishes were unimportant in the larger scheme of things. She became furious and started yelling at him.

Dr. Jerry, who'd been listening from his bed, jumped on the couch and settled himself between them. This stopped the argument and they asked some questions like, "How did he know to do that?" and "Does he do that with every couple?" They wondered out loud if I'd trained him to do that, which I hadn't.

Soon enough, Tom and Mary realized that Dr. Jerry had diverted their attention and calmed them down. They went on to a better discussion about the problem. Mary explained how the dirty dishes made her nerves jangle, and Tom said he'd been working on a family budget he considered more important. The session ended with them having a real conversation rather than their typical argument. Now I had their buy-in on how animal-assisted couples therapy might be different—since they'd said I was their last hope.

At the next session, Tom began by criticizing Mary for continuing her online friendships with old boyfriends. He did so in an attacking way—she was inconsiderate; she couldn't be trusted; she was needy; and she was selfish! Mary's response was to counterat-

DR. JERRY AND COUPLES

tack. She cut him off and then threw the proverbial kitchen sink at Tom, bringing up every transgression he'd ever committed going back to their dating years. Dr. Jerry listened attentively and looked to me for a cue. I sort of nodded, and he promptly jumped between them.

Having interrupted this totally ineffective way of communicating, I had Tom start over and share his feelings about Mary's Facebook behavior. This time, rather that tell Mary about Mary ("you" messages), he told Mary about Tom ("I" messages). He said her continuing these old relationships made him feel sad, hurt, and scared. When she invalidated him and told him he shouldn't feel that way, I pointed out how she did this and how it only caused Tom more pain. I coached her to share more authentically and less defensively. She said she felt lonely because he wouldn't listen to her and connect with her...and her old boyfriends did! Tom connected the dots and vowed to step up by doing more housework and also by being a more attentive listener.

Old patterns are hard to change. At the next session, Tom and Mary avoided any real issues between them, talking about a trip she'd made, an issue he'd had at work, and so on. I said I was interested in what was happening in the room and how they were doing since our last session, when Tom had promised to change. That blew the lid off and an argument ensued, the most vicious yet, over who was suffering more. Once again, Dr. Jerry had to jump between them to call attention to the pointlessness of their way of relating and to defuse the tension. This time they laughed and asked if they could take Dr. Jerry home.

I refused the request but told them they could internalize Dr. Jerry and imagine he was there when an argument was spinning out of control. I think I joked about getting a Dr. Jerry cutout made, but they understood the point. The old way didn't work—they'd tried it for fifteen years! This was a turning point. After this, they got better at sharing airtime and became more skillful about showing up with authentic feelings rather than complaints about the other. This allowed me to do some psychoeducational work and teach them listening skills, disengaging skills, negotiating skills and, above all, supportive skills. Dr. Jerry and I now had their attention.

Somewhere around the tenth session I convinced Tom and Mary, or they convinced themselves, that it is easier and far less effective to complain than to ask for what one wants. Besides, every time they did it the old way, an argument would ensue, and Dr. Jerry would have to get out of bed and jump between them. Once they got the wisdom of stating a request versus making a complaint, their communication improved dramatically.

I also taught them to ask the question "How can I support you?" Just hearing a caring partner ask that simple question without trying to solve the problem can often be all the other needs. And if they need more, they can say, "Please just listen," or "I'd like a hug," or "It would mean a lot to me if you'd vacuum the house today."

As simple as this seems, Tom and Mary had trouble hearing it or taking it in. They both resisted it, probably because there were still old resentments in the way. To bypass their defenses, I told them I was going to have an out-loud consultation session with Dr. Jerry. They were to listen in, which got them out of the automatic pattern of resisting. I turned and spoke directly to the dog. I said, "Dr. Jerry, when I coach Tom and Mary to ask each other for support rather than complain about not getting it, they won't take it in. I don't know what this is about, but I'd love to see them do an experiment for two weeks by trying it and then reporting back." That was all I said.

At the next session I inquired about the proposed homework. Happily, Tom and Mary tried it and quickly realized it worked better than their old communication pattern. When we were finished with therapy, they were doing a much better job communicating, negotiating, listening, accepting differences, and accepting each other's influence. Mary still communicates with old boyfriends but validates Tom's feelings about it (they see it differently and accept that). Dr. Jerry was very much a part of teaching these skills, especially in the early sessions when he sat between them to call attention to how they fought so unfairly and ineffectively. His diversion was like a reset button that set the stage for them to build awareness, make better choices, and grow.

I don't understand people who don't touch their pets. Their cat or dog is called a pet for a reason.
—Jarod Kintz

The family—Katherine, Bill, Diana, and the dogs—Jenny, Dr. Jerry, and Jack

26

DR. JERRY AND JACK WITH FAMILIES WHO ATTACK

Dr. Jerry and Jack form a winning combination when working with families who present with anger management or domestic violence issues. This holds true whether we're meeting in my office or doing a home visit. In either case, as always, I get family consent first. If it's a home visit, I make sure there isn't a dog in the home that might be territorial. I've noticed that pet owners with anger problems often have dogs with the same bad habits. What a coincidence!

First I establish that anger is indeed the primary issue (as opposed to alcoholism or a mental illness such as bipolar disorder) and that the family in question truly understands how corrosive anger is to their happiness and life satisfaction. If they're motivated to change by learning to express anger more effectively, it's ten times more productive than if I'm lecturing them and trying to change them into nice people—which is an exercise in futility, because it inevitably leads to resistance. It reminds me of an old saying…"Never try to teach a pig to sing. It never works and it only pisses off the pig!"

If we have a contract to learn to handle anger in a skillful way, then I bring up the idea of using the dogs. Note that I don't try to put an end to the anger, as it's often an appropriate and healthy response to what's happening. If a husband is cheating, the wife is entitled to be hurt and angry. If the wife is critical and contemptuous of her husband, he has a right to be hurt, sad and angry. If the parents are punitive and using corporal punishment, the kids have a right to be angry. What I want to accomplish is for families to use anger in ways that create positive changes rather than retaliatory acting out.

I introduce Dr. Jerry and Jack as sensitive and caring animals who need to be treated with gentleness, respect, and goodwill. I explain that the dogs will be expected to show good boundaries and will be held accountable if they slip. Implied in my presentation is that the family we're working with deserves no less. This sets the stage for how the family will learn to communicate with one another, as well as how they will deal with important issues such as boundary setting and accountability. This is all new to some families, especially those who harm one another with angry words and actions.

The Johnsons came to treatment referred by another therapist, who saw the wife individually. They had a rebellious daughter who experimented with drugs and underperformed academically. Differences in parenting styles (he played bad guy to her good guy) created a great deal of extra stress in their lives, and it led to some ugly fights with threats of divorce. There was no domestic violence, though the mother grew up with it and was always afraid her husband would snap. The daughter seemed like a good kid who was starved for attention and got her sense of belonging by acting out with peers.

About four sessions in, the daughter called the mother a "selfish *c-word*" in my office. Having worked in prisons, I'm used to bad language, but I admit to being shocked. Mom flew into an instant rage and lashed out at her daughter without the slightest interest in what was behind the abusive words. Dad chimed in on Mom's side with some name-calling of his own, though not on the daughter's scale. I stepped in and asked for a time-out to allow everyone to collect themselves. This was going nowhere, although it was exactly what they did at home so useful for me to observe first-hand.

I then invited the family to pet and hold Dr. Jerry and Jack, as long as it was one at a time. Gently focusing on the dogs proved soothing to all and gave them a chance to regulate their emotions and reset their nervous systems from stress response to relaxation response, or at least in that direction. With the energy in the room more conducive to real communication, I pointed out to the mother that she wasn't even curious about why her daughter was so angry. As she had calmed down, she was now able to see her daughter had a point. She had a right to be angry because her mother had put the family in dire financial straits by spending money carelessly, which resulted in not enough money for new school clothes for her daughter.

I underlined for the daughter that her anger was valid, but the way she chose to express it was shocking and inappropriate. I told the teen that it not only was disrespectful and hurtful to her mother to talk that way, but bad for her. The daughter would soon go into the world and needed to learn to express herself in a more mature way. She claimed it was the only way she could get her mother to listen, and I was inclined to believe her. Still, unacceptable! I helped her to see that her mother didn't listen, only retaliated.

Next I explained that when the dogs act out or break the rules, there must be a consequence, or else there's no learning. I said that if one of the dogs became aggressive to the other, he would be tied up on a short leash for some period of time. This teaches accountability.

Dad said to Mom that if the dogs were held to such a standard, they certainly should hold their daughter to one. They agreed and took away their daughter's cell phone (in front of me), which generated some histrionics but (I learned later) stopped any further use of that foul word.

In subsequent sessions, the Johnsons bonded with Dr. Jerry and Jack and learned to lower their voices and really listen to one another. Most of the time the dogs would be in someone's lap or by their side, a reminder to the family to be gentle and respectful to one another. Helping to generalize this learning to the home, the family adopted two adorable Pug dogs—a constant reminder to use anger appropriately and to disengage quickly if something flared up. I don't recommend this to every family (and didn't to them), but for some families a pet is a way to defuse tension for all. Still, families must learn and use skills.

Sadly, the Johnsons lost their home as they couldn't make payments and had to move into a small apartment. This created more stress, and they reverted back to fighting disrespectfully. At the next session, I brought in a very small dog bed—one that's a tight fit for the boys. I invited the family to watch how Dr. Jerry and Jack work out the space problem.

Predictably, Jack jumped directly into the bed, since he always has to be first. Dr. Jerry walked around the edge of the bed and didn't force his way in. Instead, he waited until Jack got up to get a drink of water and then slipped in. Jack came back and climbed in, and they figured out a way both of them can share the bed at the same time. Once they snuggled up together, they fell asleep and began to snore contentedly.

The family commented on Dr. Jerry's patience and equanimity. They also felt that if the dogs could share a tight space and be harmonious, they could too. We talked about patience and listening as key skills for the art of communication. This demonstration also gave the mother an opportunity to see how, like Jack, she had to be first, had to win, had to be the center of attention. I think she was a little embarrassed to see herself in the actions of a dog, but it worked to raise her awareness. "Don't be like Jack!" the daughter would playfully remind her mother.

The Johnsons ended therapy with new communication skill-sets that included mutual gentleness and respect, real listening, appropriate expressions of anger, negotiating, boundary setting, accountability, sharing space, and so much more. The dogs had a paw in all of it.

My little dogs…heartbeats at my feet.
—Edith Wharton

Aunt Annabel with Jenny and Dr. Jerry

27

WORKING WITH THE ELDERLY

✳ ✳ ✳

Animal-assisted therapy with the elderly is known to have multiple benefits. I use my dogs to visit those confined in nursing homes or assisted living situations, as well as elders who are able to make it to my office. The benefits have been confirmed by research and include lower levels of stress, improved socialization, better interpersonal relationships, enhanced self-esteem, and symptom alleviation in those with dementia.

At one nursing home I visited, the staff told me that the dogs were very helpful when it came to getting their residents to talk. Even residents who have become withdrawn and isolated will brighten up and verbalize when they play with the dogs. Touching and petting the dogs works like magic in getting them to share about their lives, the pets they've known and loved, and interesting stories from the past.

Nothing lights up the face of a senior citizen more than introducing a cuddly dog to their arms and laps. Some say they never thought they'd see a dog again and become emotional as they remember dogs they've loved and shared their lives with. They see dogs as important sources of companionship, and visits by Dr. Jerry, Jack, and Jenny remind them of those connections. Conversations ensue that reinforce their attachment to pets they've had and to other residents who've had pets in their lives. This increases their sense of friendship and belonging with other residents. And reminiscing about pets gives them a positive way to reconnect with themselves.

I recall a nursing home I visited without the dogs because I was checking it out, letting them check me out, and deciding if it would be a good fit. When Martha, age ninety-one, learned I had three therapy dogs she exacted a promise that I bring them soon, and staff consented. She then proceeded to tell all the residents that three Brussels Griffons were coming on a particular day. On the day we arrived, Martha waited expectantly at the front door. The dogs were greeted with warm hugs and bountiful love, and it was clear she didn't want them to ever leave. They licked her, wagged their tails, and competed for who was going to get the most attention (Jack won).

After that our visits became quite a social event. Martha loved to play "show and tell" around the nursing home. We visited all over the facility, and other residents would ooh and aah over the dogs while Martha beamed with satisfaction. The experience got everyone talking, laughing, and sharing about all kinds of things, but especially dog stories. Staff members told me they'd never seen Martha or other residents so engaged and happy and encouraged me and the dogs to visit on a regular basis.

We did, and Dr. Jerry, Jack, and Jenny made lots of good new friends. They even learned the phrase, "Let's go see Martha." They would jump up and down and run in circles, barking their little heads off. They would also run up the stairs to the bed so I could put on their matching coats without requiring me to bend over. Martha loved to take off their coats and then put them back on as if she was playing with dolls. All three dogs loved this kind of attention.

Our visits helped Martha and the other residents come alive and share their stories of animals they'd had in their lives. Elders love to reminisce, and it's good for them, so there was a therapeutic benefit to this. I also noticed the dogs helped to improve everyone's mood and decrease their sense of loneliness. Those who petted and played with them came away feeling more calm and grounded. These little bundles of joy are a real treasure to all whom they meet, but no one seems to appreciate them more than senior citizens who no longer live at home with access to pets.

Ode to My Dog

Because of you,
someone is always
joyous when I
return home.
Because of you,
I am
never cold
when I lie
on the floor.
Because of you,
the click of a lock
is greeted by a jingling of metal tags.
Because of you,
I am
forced
to run around and play.
Because of you,
one hug
makes everything
seem a little better.
You are always there,
you always love me.
You never talk back,
and you always forgive.
You are special,
you understand me
better then anyone.
You calm me down
and make me reasonable.
I love you
with all my heart.
—Wise Wilson

Dr. Jerry makes me smile

28

THE CHALLENGE OF WORKING WITH TEENS

Having worked as a probation officer for fifteen years, I have a great deal of experience working with teenagers. I enjoy this work because they face a time that is both challenging and crucial in terms of their family, social, and academic lives. There is a window that's open, and there's still time to get through it, but if they don't make some changes, that window may close. Once that happens, their prospects are decidedly lower.

Typically, teens show up for therapy under pressure from concerned parents, frustrated teachers, or the juvenile court system. They rarely come voluntarily and most often don't want to be in my office, don't want to be in treatment, and don't want to talk about their problems or what's going on in their chaotic lives.

Because they are "told" to see a therapist, they most often come with a rebellious attitude that pretty much guarantees resistance to change. And they seemingly dare you to reject them as they display their assortment of bad or socially unacceptable behaviors.

As I look back on my experiences with teens, the most common problems are changes in the family such as separation or divorce, trauma inflicted by either parents or parents' significant others, substance abuse, being bullied at school, personal or gender identity, and teen pregnancy. These kinds of stresses result in depression, drastic mood or personality changes, suicidal ideas (or actions), eating disorders, school behavior problems (truancy, acting out), academic failure, high-risk sexual behavior, non-suicidal self-injurious behavior (cutting), video game addiction, running away, and violence.

Yikes! You might wonder why any counselor would want to take on problems of that magnitude, but I love the challenge of working with the angry rebel part of their personalities. After an initial consultation I bring in Jack and set the stage by telling them how he's a rebel who likes to test boundaries. My young clients see this in him right away, and they love it. They see his self-absorbed, cocky attitude, and I believe they must identify with him. Even the toughest, angriest teen who refuses to talk finds himself opening up, talking about how cool Jack is, and then eventually about his own life.

Making Jack my co-therapist changes the way teens see me. They arrive expecting that I will be stuffy and close minded and follow a traditional doctor-patient kind of relationship, talking down to them or lecturing them. Generally speaking, they don't think an adult is capable of understanding what they're going through or that we're capable of genuine dialogue. They think I'm going to define them as "the problem" and try to change them according to some kind of cookie-cutter grown-up agenda (e.g., do your homework, don't do drugs, eat your vegetables, be nice to your sister). Seeing me present myself as a real person and watching me interact with Jack changes all this. It bypasses their resistance so that they can become agents of change, reaching their own goals—which may even mean they choose to do their homework, avoid drugs, eat healthfully, and act nicer!

Some therapies with teens fail because the therapist is hiding behind a role and then coming across as a control freak or a phony. Because teens have a built-in BS detector, this provides them with the perfect excuse to shut down and put no effort into the treatment process. With Jack in the room, I think I appear more human and authentic. They see me play with him, we laugh, we tell stories, we share our imperfections and vulnerabilities—it's more like I'm a wise mentor or a good coach than a strict parent or "headshrinker" who focuses on how they're messing up their lives. I try to meet with them where they are rather than judge them.

Obviously, safety is a key issue if the teen is to "speak the unspeakable" and decide to make positive changes. Jack's presence lifts some of the seriousness of the process and allows them to experience a safe place where they can learn new ways of thinking about things, new strategies to cope with intense feelings, and improved approaches for relating to family, peers, and teachers. Eventually almost all my teen clients mention that they felt safe to say what's so for them without being judged, criticized, or punished. A big part of this safety factor was the energy in the room as a result of Jack's involvement and their interaction with him.

Take the case of Jack...yes, that was his name, and he loved the fact that my Jack had the same name. For clarity, I'll call the dog "little Jack," as that is what I sometimes call him at home. Jack the client was a troubled sixteen-year-old with a lot of adverse childhood experiences (ACES). His parents had divorced; Dad abandoned him and his siblings; Mom had substance abuse issues; he had endured physical abuse under the guise of discipline; and he also witnessed domestic violence inflicted upon his mother. It's virtually impossible to suffer this much trauma and not have mental health problems.

Jack had recently moved, he had no friends, he displayed angry outbursts in school, and he was continually fighting with his mother and siblings. He was severely depressed and felt hopeless about his life. He was also self-medicating with alcohol and smoking tobacco and marijuana. When we factor in how all these negative experiences and drug abuse would affect his developing brain, it's no wonder he was in trouble!

Referred by the juvenile justice system (shoplifting, street drugs, fistfights at school), Jack arrived at my office as angry as could be and refusing to talk. I invited him to sit on the floor with little Jack. Jack decided it would be okay and maybe even fun to play, and he threw the ball for little Jack and held him and laughed. He shared that he had not laughed in a long time. Little Jack rolled over, did the army crawl, sat up like a bunny, and did his high five. He endeared himself to Jack, and the therapy took off.

At the next session, little Jack climbed onto Jack's chest and licked his face. I began to ask a few non-threatening questions about his life. Out came lots of information—mostly about the aforementioned ACES. All the while Jack was petting little Jack slowly on his head and his stomach. Tears came, and little Jack licked them off of his cheeks. Clearly, Jack wanted and needed to vent his feelings in a safe environment, and I gave him kudos for taking the risk. This led to a discussion of the office as a safe place where he could share without being judged or criticized. I heard his story and supported him with compassion and validation. I let him know I felt honored to hear what had happened to him and how it affected him currently. At the end of every session, Jack made sure I would have little Jack present at the next one. I reassured him he could work with little Jack whenever he came in. Trust developed far more quickly than if I was going it alone.

I also brought in Dr. Jerry when we began talking about more mature behavior and making wiser choices. I set the stage by telling Jack that Dr. Jerry has a lot of patience and better impulse control than little Jack. Jack believed me and would look into Dr. Jerry's eyes when exploring what wisdom was about. Jack learned to wait and think things through rather than acting on impulse alone. He learned to talk and act in more respectful ways, even when he was angry. He appreciated that I validated his anger—that he was entitled to be angry. At the same time, I urged him to find more skillful and effective ways to express it.

Over time, Jack processed his feelings about being physically abused and the shame and rage he felt. Little Jack, Dr. Jerry, and I listened to his story and supported him. Eventually he realized he'd been powerless to stop it; he was a victim who'd done nothing wrong. The perpetrator was the one who should carry the shame, not he. This was emotional work, and the dogs could always sense when Jack was in pain. He appreciated the extra attention they would give him during such vulnerable moments. Jack said he felt less alone, and I could see him rebuilding his wounded self-esteem or, possibly, building it in a positive way for the first time. He came to believe something bad had happened to him rather than thinking he was a bad person!

Progress led to letting go of his grievances and to forgiveness for the one who abused him. This allowed Jack to move on and take responsibility for writing a new chapter in his life. He wanted a dog of his own, adopted one from a shelter, and took excellent care of her. He began participating in sports and attended several clubs at school, which gave him a sense of belonging. Step by step he carried out his new plan for life, and his self-confidence grew leaps and bounds. He made friends outside the drug culture and hung out with them after school. His depression lifted, and he felt hope for the future.

Jack still calls from time to time to say hi and to let me know how he's doing. He attends college out of state and is pursuing a career in science (though he is open to other possibilities, including becoming a counselor who uses dogs to assist the therapy process). He now lives a balanced life with good self-care and is free of all addiction. He does well in school and has built a supportive group of friends. He accepts his family-of-origin as dysfunctional but doesn't allow himself to get sucked into their ongoing drama. I feel so blessed to have watched Jack turn his life around and know I couldn't have done it without little Jack and Dr. Jerry.

Dogs have a way of finding the people who need them and filling an emptiness we didn't even know we had.
—Unknown

Batman…the owner of my editor, Stan

29

BATMAN SAVES THE DAY

My editor, Stan, has a five-year-old French Bulldog who accompanies him to work. He started taking him because he and his wife were remodeling, and Batman, being sensitive, didn't like all the strangers in his space. When the remodel ended, Stan stopped bringing Batman and received a chorus of unanimous protests from his clients. That was several years ago, and Batman is now a fixture at work.

Stan told me a story I would like to share. Batman is not a certified therapy dog, but he is therapeutic with Stan's clients, as indicated by his eventual effect on Jillian, a teenage girl with serious depression and suicidal impulses. She professed to not like dogs and barely tolerated Batman's gentle attempts to befriend her. In fact, Jillian was withdrawn and moody with everyone she met or knew, including family.

Sadly, Jillian made a serious suicide attempt and nearly completed it. She ended up in the hospital in a coma from an overdose, and when she recovered she went directly to a psychiatric hospital for another month. Stan visited her in the hospital and told her, in essence, that her problem was that she thought there was something wrong with her and consequently wouldn't let any love in. He cited her parents and her sister as examples of people who love her but who she shuts out. He went on to point out how he and Batman were both fond of her, but she wouldn't allow either to get close. Jillian made the connection that getting close made her feel vulnerable and that she was afraid of getting hurt.

When Jillian returned to Stan's office for therapy for the first time in six weeks, Batman greeted her like a long-lost friend. He jumped up on the couch, got on her lap, and licked her neck and cheeks. Stan asked if she wanted him to get Batman to stop. Jillian said no and let it continue. Then she joked, "I might as well give you my check for the session now, because I've gotten exactly what I needed."

I know Batman; he is shy, so this was uncharacteristic for him. Jillian asked if he did this for all Stan's clients, and he told her that she was hands down the dog's favorite. They proceeded to discuss how something had changed in the hospital. She said she could take the risk of letting Batman give her love, as he asked for nothing in return. As we've heard before, it felt safe to let in a dog's love. Because of this, she decided she liked dogs after all.

Jillian decided to get a dog and with her parents' blessings rescued one from a local shelter. She reported it was easier to accept a pet's love as it was easier to trust them. Her new dog, a female Shepherd mix she named Luna, was a sweetheart, and the two bonded quickly. They started running and hiking together, and Jillian took Luna to an obedience class. Luna gave Jillian something to live for (her words), as well as a source and an object of love. Jillian was also the person solely responsible for Luna's care, and this inspired her to also take better care of herself.

Jillian still sees Stan and her life is dramatically different. She loves Luna and lets in her doggy love. Her depression lifted and her self-esteem improved. She decided she wanted to live, and she wanted to do it in a loving way. She started going to church voluntarily, she has a boyfriend, she is closer with her parents, sister, and friends. According to Jillian, all these changes started with Batman's unconditional love, affection, and her newfound ability to let it in.

A person can learn a lot from a dog, even a loopy one like ours. Marley taught me about living each day with unbridled exuberance and joy, about seizing the moment and following your heart. He taught me to appreciate the simple things—a walk in the woods, a fresh snowfall, a nap in a shaft of winter sunlight. And as he grew old and achy, he taught me about optimism in the face of adversity. Mostly, he taught me about friendship and selflessness and above all else, unwavering loyalty.

—John Grogan

Diana with Jenny, Dr. Jerry, and Jack on the farm

30

MINDFULNESS AND
THE DOGS

❁ ❁ ❁

Animals in general, and dogs in particular, live a present-centered life and therefore remind us to live in the moment. This is a key element in being mindful, which is an emerging and important concept in successful psychotherapies of all kinds. Mindfulness, the centerpiece of Buddhist Psychology for over two thousand years, is here defined as paying attention to whatever is happening in the present moment and doing it without judgment.

Western research, particularly the disciplines of Acceptance and Commitment Therapy and Dialectical Behavior Therapy, have shown mindfulness to be effective in reducing depression and anxiety, lowering stress levels, and improving emotional regulation.

Mindfulness is easily adaptable to pet-assisted therapy and a goal of mine in my work with clients.

My therapy dogs teach me and my clientele to be aware of what is going on around us, to stand still and experience the sensations that arise in our bodies, and to attend to the constant barrage of thoughts that seemingly never cease. Like our canine friends, we can learn to see, smell, touch, taste, and hear our environment with fewer judgments. For example, and I take the liberty of an assumption here, my dogs might say, "It's rainy and cold out today." Humans turn it into a story via their judgments, so it becomes, "It's miserable out...I can't stand this weather." It is the stories we tell ourselves about our experience that make us miserable, not the experience itself. Our minds are not necessarily our friends. If we can learn to accept what is, we've won half the battle.

Mindfulness is a state of active, open attention to the present, and this is what dogs do better than we—the two-legged mammals—do. I observe my dogs doing that in my practice. Having a dog sit on your lap, or taking them for a walk and noticing how they see, smell, feel energy, hear, and touch, teaches us to be mindful. They sense more and think less.

In the office, the dogs show mindfulness by attending to the moment with the client, the counselor, and the process of therapy (voice tones and levels, body language, facial expressions, emotional expression). Unless they're sleeping (when not much is happening and I don't need them), the dogs focus on what's going on with the humans, and what's going on between the humans. They keep an eye on me to make sure they're doing what I want them to be doing, and the rest is attending to the moment with whatever is taking place.

Mark came into the office for a scheduled appointment and reported he had had a horrible day at work. His boss had gotten after him, his coworkers had been unfairly critical, and his clients had made unrealistic demands. He felt depressed, anxious, and overwhelmed emotionally.

Dr. Jerry picked up on Mark's mood, sat at his feet, and asked to get into his lap. Mark noticed the request and invited him up. They sat together and while Mark filled in the details of his bad day, he gave the "Good Doctor" smooth strokes across his back. He also scratched under Dr. Jerry's chin, ears, and gently stroked his belly. In a matter of minutes, Mark calmed down, centered himself in the present moment, and let go of his negative energy about the day. So much of what people really want is about safety and about feeling loved. Dr. Jerry provides both, and he does it unconditionally.

This connection with Dr. Jerry helped Mark to detach from all the drama and look at his problems without judgment. He was able to take responsibility for his part of the problem at work and to not take the rest so personally. He acknowledged he couldn't have done this in the emotional state he suffered at the beginning of the session. Dr. Jerry provided a soothing presence that allowed Mark to regulate his emotions and deal with his day.

From then on, Mark entered the session room and promptly placed Dr. Jerry on his lap. He called Dr. Jerry his "Guru," because he helped him center himself quickly. Mark went on to learn meditation, he began a program of daily walking, he ate more consciously and chose healthful food. He noticed how self-critical he was and used more positive self-talk. His depression and anxiety lifted. He started sleeping well and could now manage his moods in ways that no longer affected his outlook on life. He gave Dr. Jerry credit for teaching him to be less reactive under stress.

Another example comes to mind. Jane brought in her boyfriend, Phil, wanting to learn how to de-escalate when they fought, which was often. My initial interview with them showed that they were not practicing mindfulness. They had almost no awareness of what they were fighting over, no awareness of what they wanted from the other, no skills in how to communicate their wants or needs, and typically blamed each other for their problems without any awareness of their own part in the fighting. Moreover, they were super judgmental of one another ("he's clueless and controlling," "she's overemotional and crazy"). Both Jane and Phil were convinced that they had the one correct view of reality, and the other was simply wrong. They mistakenly thought I would declare the winner.

After watching Jane and Phil fight and get nowhere, I said something to the effect that we knew that what they were doing now didn't work. It might be a good idea to try another approach. I convinced them to let me bring in Jack and Dr. Jerry because I believed they would bring down the anger level so we could at least start a meaningful dialogue. They agreed, and the next session found them with the two dogs on their laps—Dr. Jerry with Jane, and Jack with Phil. How the dogs chose I cannot say, but I imagine they read unconscious energy. Petting the dogs had the immediate effect of calming both clients, which in turn allowed them to listen better to each other. The dogs were sweet and affectionate, and this made it easier for me to do some psychoeducational work and teach Jane and Phil communication and relationship skills. It's actually quite difficult to rage at someone when an adorable and attentive dog is giving you love. The dogs provided me a captive and attentive audience.

I pointed out how different the two dogs are (Dr. Jerry a gentle, people pleaser and Jack a rebel through and through), yet they get along splendidly because they don't insist their way is the right way. They simply accept one another without trying to change the other. Jane and Phil were sent home with homework to practice, most notably allowing differences to stand rather than yelling at each other as if that way, they could get the other to come over to their way of seeing things.

In a few sessions, with the dogs' help, Jane and Phil did much better listening to each other, remained calm most of the time, de-escalated when stress levels got too high, and learned to negotiate whenever possible. What allowed them to make these changes was improved mindfulness, which could only happen after they relaxed a bit. They were more aware of what was happening between them, more aware of their own bodily cues and thoughts, and more present to the moment rather than stuck in angry patterns that had never worked. The dogs truly helped them find ways to stay present-centered and without the judgments that demonized the other. They didn't always agree with one another, but they disagreed more skillfully and respectfully – just as Dr. Jerry and Jack did.

Spiritual fulfillment doesn't have to mean belief in a religion or disbelief in science...whether one believes in a unseen, all-knowing force, or the wonder of science and the universe, or simply the beauty of the human spirit, nearly everyone of us feels an inner longing to feel part of something bigger than ourselves.

—Cesar Millan

Dr. Jerry basking in the sun and embracing life

31

THE DOGS AND
SPIRITUAL DIRECTION

❋ ❋ ❋

When I work as a Spiritual Director, I begin with an assumption—namely, dogs are spirits just as we are. Therefore it is no surprise to me that my therapy dogs respond to the energy and emotion in the office when clients are working on spiritual issues. This comes up whenever clients have an issue with their Higher Power or God that involves anger, shame, fear, feelings of abandonment or betrayal, and so on. Unfortunately, many clients have been abused by people who claim to be religious and tend to sour against religion or God.

My approach is to have clients dialogue with God when they are struggling with such a spiritual issue or with another kind of problem that might have a spiritual solution. The goal of these conversations is to have the client reach a deeper understanding, an acceptance of whatever is happening, an improved relationship with God, or a letting go in a way that brings them greater peace. Just as I feel something changing the energy in the room, the dogs feel it too, and they play a key role in this spiritual work. I don't know how they do this, but I believe they sense the shift in energy and respond appropriately.

I wish I knew exactly how the dogs experience these subtle changes, but I don't. I'll say this—it is uncanny how they tune in empathetically to my clients. This then motivates the dogs to either sit next to the client or get in their lap, assuming it's not too intrusive. If clients become emotional and cry, the dogs will lick the tears from their cheeks (as long as they get a go-ahead). The dogs know this is not always okay and look to me and the client for permission. Here are some stories to demonstrate how the dogs and I collaborate to do spiritual direction.

Susan had a long and chaotic drug and alcohol history. She felt deep shame over choices she'd made while in the throes of addiction. Most of it centered around sexual promiscuity that happened over a span of five years. She reported difficulty attending AA meetings and doing her Twelve-Step work because she believed God did not love her. In her mind, Susan believed her past sexual behavior made her unforgivable. Her fourth step ("make a searching and fearless moral inventory of ourselves") seemed impossible to Susan because it meant exposing her sexual choices and facing judgment (her own and others'). She arrived at therapy after reaching an impasse, this despite regular AA meetings and support from a competent sponsor.

I gave her my rationale and got her permission to bring in Dr. Jerry. Her homework had been to make a list of what she wanted to talk to God about, and she had a written list with her. As planned, Dr. Jerry got in her lap, and we led Susan into guided imagery with God. She imagined being with God and described how it felt to be in his presence using words like "peaceful," "blissful," and "awe-inspiring." Meanwhile, Dr. Jerry purred in her lap (Brussels Griffons make a purring noise when sleeping and being stroked). She presented her dilemma to God and got back the message that He had always loved her and that she'd already been forgiven.

Susan seemed oblivious to Dr. Jerry but kept stroking him and went into a deep trancelike state. Here, she got a message from God that He understood her sexual acting-out to be based on a need for love and attention. He also "told" her she deserved to be loved as a little girl, even though she didn't get it from her caretakers. This knowledge elicited deep, racking sobs that came from way down inside Susan's body. The energy shifted in the room, and Dr. Jerry woke up. He immediately looked to me to see if it was okay to lick her tears, and I gave him a nod. This gave Susan great comfort, as she took Dr. Jerry's nurturing love at the same time she took in the feeling she was loved and forgiven by God.

Susan went on to ask God if He would be there for her when she did her Twelve-Step work. She reported confidently that God would always be there and support her and that she would never have to be alone again. Dr. Jerry stayed with her until the moment our session ended. He followed her to the door and out into the waiting room to the top of the steps that led down to the front door. She commented on how Dr. Jerry had facilitated the work and that she wished she could take him home. I told her he was in her heart now, and she could take him everywhere she goes.

Another case comes to mind. Janet, a single, middle-aged professional, came into therapy to deal with an eating disorder—habitual overeating leading to obesity. Our first interview showed she had unfinished business from being molested as a child. Her belief was that God must not love her or he would have been there to protect her from the trauma that shaped her life. Why, she asked, did God not stop the years of abuse she had endured? Janet had stopped attending church because she thought God abandoned her, and on top of that, she felt dirty and tainted. She became rebellious as a teen as a way of acting out her identity as a bad girl.

I brought Jack to the office to help with Janet, having already suggested that she think about what she would like to say to God. She smiled when I told her Jack was a rebel, knowing they might share that character trait. After playing together and bonding, Jack settled down in her lap. Janet set the stage by imagining talking to God in her old church and bringing along her childhood dog, Sam.

As a way of beginning the guided imagery, I asked her to visualize herself as a child. She asked God why He had abandoned her and whether He ever loved her. She reported that God said He was always there for her but that He allows bad things to happen because man has free will and has strayed from His Word. As an example, He even allowed Jesus to be humiliated and crucified.

God acknowledged that He allowed her parents and brothers to do what they did, but that the sin was with them, not her. He also reassured her He would help her to get through her work now, including a new way of looking at things to show Janet she'd done nothing wrong and there was nothing to be forgiven.

In a subsequent session with Jack again on her lap, Janet discovered that God was a loving God. He helped her find compassion and forgiveness for her family, and at the same time she could protect herself from any further victimization, whether sexual or emotional. She commented that God's love for her was like Jack's— unconditional and without judgment. For the first time in her life, she felt deserving of love. God "told" her she could go ahead and feel joy and happiness now for her "child within her." She understood her family had harmed her out of their own wounds, not because of any badness or shame within her character or being. This in no way excused their hurtful actions, but did help explain them. Janet learned to love and protect herself while at the same time holding her family accountable.

During these sessions when Janet spoke with God, I sat and witnessed. When the energy shifted in the room, Jack would lick her hand, put his little feet on her chest, and look her straight in the eye as if to say, "I understand and feel both your pain and relief." Janet would cry hard and then collect herself by stroking Jack. He stayed with Janet until she finished her imagery work and then walked with her through the waiting room to the top of the stairs. He stood and watched her to say good-bye. Perhaps he wished to assure her that he would see her again soon.

When we terminated treatment, Janet had gotten a handle on her eating disorder because she'd learned to regulate her negative emotions without food. (When I "terminate" a client I assure them that I will always save a seat for them so they know they could return if they needed further counseling from me and the dogs.) She credited Jack for showing her how she could soothe herself without diving into the refrigerator. Instead, she reached out to friends, prayed, meditated, journaled, and exercised. She said Jack worked like glue for her to hold herself together and practice better self-care.

WHAT IS SPIRITUAL DIRECTION?

❋ ❋ ❋

Spiritual direction helps develop others' awareness of connection to God or a Higher Power so they can live more peacefully, forgive others, develop a heart of compassion, be less judgmental, stand for justice, and be imbued with a healing presence. It takes place when a person voluntarily seeks out a professional or trained Spiritual Director, defined here as a person who possesses a mature theological knowledge, who is moved by the Holy Spirit, and who is dedicated to God. The seeker or directee desires a deeper relationship with the spiritual aspects of being. Successful direction helps the seeker to integrate what they've learned about their own spirituality into their everyday life.

Spiritual direction differs from psychotherapy or counseling in that the latter focuses on psychological problems and learning to cope effectively, whereas spiritual direction focuses on becoming more intimate with God. I think of psychotherapy as being primarily about the mind and body; spiritual direction is more about the heart and the soul. Spiritual direction can be an aspect of psychotherapy and counseling can be an aspect of spiritual direction, but they are not the same disciplines.

An example: Cindy, a trauma survivor, had successful counseling with a specialist who used research-proven techniques to help her let go of fear, resolve grief, and move on with her life. She came to me because she wanted additional help to deal with some unanswered spiritual issues. Our work involved prayer, a focus on forgiveness for herself and for the man who had traumatized her, as well as a strengthening of her belief that God is always good and always loves her, even when He allows bad things to happen. In the end, Cindy even found compassion for her assailant. (Note: this is in no way whatsoever excusing his criminal behavior.) My intention in such a case is to serve as a spiritually aware listener helping directees develop spiritual discernment, which will be defined later.

This case showed how counseling and spiritual direction can complement one another—where one leaves off, the other begins. I might even go so far as to say that both counseling and spiritual direction are ideal, but not sufficient standing alone. This isn't always true, but it was with Cindy, who used an unfortunate and terrifying life event to deepen her relationship and commitment to God and to grow as a spiritual being.

The following list will demonstrate what constitutes spiritual direction, and clarify what Spiritual Directors actually do:

1. Spiritual direction is an interpersonal relationship in which we learn how to grow, live, and love as a human spirit or soul.

2. Spiritual direction involves a process through which one person helps another person understand what God is doing and saying, even when it may appear that God is not paying attention or is indifferent, for example, when it appears that prayers are not being answered or that the answer is no.

3. Spiritual direction relies on the gift of discernment, or the ability to see beyond one's circumstances and grasp what may be obscure or undetectable to most people. Discernment can be elusive, but there is no wisdom without it.

4. Spiritual direction sessions provide a sacred space that is calm, safe, nurturing, and loving. From this place in an I-Thou relationship we talk to God or whomever we conceive our Higher Power to be.

5. The Spiritual Director gently guides another in spiritual issues through the spiritual world by spiritual means (as opposed to the psychological, material, or physical realms).

6. Spiritual direction provides another set of eyes and ears to walk beside a directee while paying attention to the movement of the Spirit within their life.

7. Spiritual Directors have a sense of being established in God or a Higher Power, an intention to walk a spiritual path, and an aim to let their light shine as an example to others.

8. Spiritual Directors respect all those who seek direction, regardless of their religious beliefs or lifestyle. As Jesus taught us, "It is not the healthy who need a doctor, but the sick. I have not come to call the righteous, but sinners" (Mark 2:17, New International Version).

9. Spiritual Directors help directees to increase awareness of the spiritual issue or issues at hand so they can make spiritually informed choices with regard to relationship problems, emotional conflicts, substance abuse, life transitions, or the perils and pitfalls of life.

10. Spiritual Directors explore and clarify values. They guide directees back onto the spiritual path when their behavior is incongruent with their deepest and most cherished values. To be happy is in large part to be aligned with one's values.

11. Spiritual Directors help directees integrate spiritual issues into their everyday lives, for example, "love thy neighbor" even if that neighbor is obnoxious, unfair, or engaged in illegal activities (which, by

the way, doesn't mean a Spiritual Director couldn't confront them skillfully or report them to the police).

12. Spiritual Directors explore priorities with directees with an eye on how they would like to live a more spiritually fulfilling life, for example, develop a more intimate relationship with God, and greater discernment as to how they are being guided by the Holy Spirit.

If you are interested in pursuing spiritual direction, seek a Spiritual Director who has been professionally trained or certified, is supervised, has a Spiritual Director of their own, and adheres to the Spiritual Directors' Code of Ethics. If you are seeking a Spiritual Director or wish to be one, visit the website www.sdiworld. org for more information. I believe the case examples given earlier in this chapter demonstrate how animal-assisted therapy and spiritual direction complement one another.

We humans may be brilliant, and we may be special, but we are still connected to the rest of life. No one reminds us of this better than our dogs. Perhaps the human condition will always include attempts to remind ourselves that we are separate from the rest of the natural world. We are different from other animals; it's undeniably true. But while acknowledging that, we must acknowledge another truth, the truth that we are also the same. That is what dogs and their emotions give us—a connection. A connection to life on Earth, to all that binds and cradles us, lest we begin to feel too alone. Dogs are our bridge—our connection to who we really are, and most tellingly, who we want to be. When we call them home to us, it's as if we are calling for home itself. And that'll do dogs. That'll do.
—Patricia B. McConnell

DR. JERRY IN PRINT

Jacqueline Crawford and Karen A. Pomerinke, *Therapy Pets: The Animal-Human Healing Partnership.* (Amherst, NY: Prometheus Books, 2003), 96–99.

Diana Lee, "Tell Dr. Jerry All About It…" *Brussels Sprouts* 31 (2002): 26.

HISTORY OF THERAPY DOGS

❂ ❂ ❂

Dogs have long been used in aiding people to deal with disabilities, heal illnesses, laugh at life's difficulties, exercise unhealthy bodies, mend lonely hearts, grieve losses, and provide emotional comfort during times of stress.

Any breed of dog is eligible to be a therapy dog (and some of the very best are mutts). All can help people grow emotionally or heal in whatever way they need to. For that matter, any animal can do the same if well trained and supportive of working with people. The stories in this book involve my therapy dogs, three Brussels Griffons who became my furry co-counselors. My dogs were certified by Delta Society, which has now become Pet Partners.

A therapy dog is trained to provide affection and comfort to people in hospitals, retirement homes, nursing homes, schools, hospices, universities, disaster areas, courts, counseling offices, and a variety of other settings.

The first official therapy dog may have been an adult female Yorkshire Terrier, found abandoned in a foxhole on a New Guinea battlefield during World War II. Corporal William Wynne bought the four-pound canine from the soldier who rescued her and named her Smoky. The dog spent a year and a half in combat at Corporal Wynne's side and became a war hero by crawling through a pipe that ran under an airstrip to reconnect a communications cable. This move allowed the airstrip to remain functional so as to ward off enemy bombing. Smoky was ultimately awarded eight battle stars.

When Corporal Wynne was hospitalized for a jungle disease, his friends brought his beloved Smoky to the hospital to provide moral support and cheer him up. The dog was at once popular and therapeutic to other ill or wounded soldiers, so he was allowed to stay with permission from the commanding officer, Dr. Charles Mayo (later of Mayo Clinic fame). After Corporal Wynne healed, Smoky would go on doctors' rounds and interact with other patients, and he did this for the next twelve years.

After learning about Smoky, a registered nurse by the name of Elaine Smith started using therapy dogs in the 1970s. She developed programs where dogs were allowed to visit hospital patients. It was noted that the dogs helped to relieve stress, improve mood, and lower blood pressure. More recently, therapy dogs have been used to help children with speech, reading issues (Reading with Rover), and emotional disorders.

Tender Loving Zoo, a nonprofit organization, was founded by Nancy Stanley in 1982. Her therapy dogs and other animals provided companionship and helped severely disabled children and the elderly in hospitals. Nancy got this idea from noticing how the disabled children loved to see the animals at the Los Angeles Zoo.

The rest is history.

Research indicates that interaction with therapy dogs, also called "animal-assisted therapy" or "pet therapy," can temporarily affect the various neurotransmitters in the brain that relate to mood. Interaction with therapy dogs elevates levels of oxytocin, a feel-good hormone that is linked with bonding and feelings of intimacy. It also raises dopamine levels, which play a major role in behaviors involving reward and motivation, important variables for anyone facing a medical or psychological crisis. Moreover, therapy dogs have been shown to relieve stress by lowering cortisol levels. To see how this works in practice, imagine a child with reading difficulties that leads to low self-esteem. Reading to a dog rather than to a person or teacher decreases self-consciousness and allows the child to relax and improve his or her reading skills.

I predict therapy dogs will become even more prevalent and useful in the years to come. For more information about certification, contact Pet Partners at www.petpartners.org.

ABOUT THE AUTHOR

❀ ❀ ❀

Diana F. Lee is an accomplished counselor with four decades of experience empowering people to resolve issues and make positive changes. She emphasizes skill building, grief work, and creativity while collaborating with other health-care professionals to facilitate improved self-esteem and a balanced, spiritually-based lifestyle.

She was born and raised in the Pacific Northwest and spent twenty-six years as a resident of Snohomish, Washington. She loves nature and, until recently, lived on a small farm that was a home for horses, goats, geese, ducks, dogs, and cats. She and her attorney husband of thirty-eight years, William, have recently moved to the "art town" of La Conner, Washington. They have a daughter, Katherine, who is also an attorney.

Diana has master's degrees in education/counseling and public administration, and a post-master's certificate in Transforming Spirituality, all from Seattle

University. She worked as a probation officer for fifteen years and has been in private practice since 1983 treating individuals, families, and couples. For the last fourteen years, she has used three Brussels Griffon as therapy dogs in her practice.

She has also completed a program in counseling chemical dependency issues and has done many years of group work with adults in addiction recovery. She is currently working as a Spiritual Director in her private practice as well. She is a local and international (Russia and China) speaker on mental health and addiction issues.

Diana is the author of *Rustproof Relationships: A Guide to Healthy Relationships and Effective Coping Skills,* and *Touching the Soul (a therapeutic guide to spiritual and personal growth).* Her fourth book, *Rustproof Relationships Revisited: A Guide to Personal Growth and Achieving Your Dreams and Goals* is to be released in winter 2016. She is currently working on a book *Loss, Renewal and Resilience.*

Diana loves to travel and has been profoundly influenced by European, Asian, and Russian cultures. With her interest in spiritual growth, Diana has visited numerous temples, churches, monasteries, and other sacred sites. A lifelong lover of horses, she has ridden in most of the countries she has visited. She has many creative outlets and has held numerous art shows that included wall hangings, photography, clothing, purses, and jewelry. She also enjoys designing gardens and homes.